Praise for *The Gospel According to Lost*

"Chris Seay is a genuine voice for a confused culture. This book will help you find your way no matter how *Lost* you may be."

Mark Batterson
Lead Pastor
National Community Church

"Chris Seay is one of my favorite people. He's a shepherd at heart. His insights on culture always take me into a better understanding of the world we live in. I'm grateful for him in so many ways."

Don Miller
Author, *Blue Like Jazz*

"I'm an enthusiastic fan of Chris Seay's work—his ability to see patterns of truth and wisdom in the artifacts of pop culture, and his desire to highlight what's good and right instead of merely lamenting what's shallow or shabby."

Brian McLaren
Author/Speaker

"Chris is not only a good friend and an innovative church planter/ leader, he is a missionary to Houston, Texas. In being a great missionary, he has lovingly told God's story through his culture's narratives. This book is a must read for people who are called to be or want to be missionaries to our 21st century cities."

Gideon Tsang
Lead Pastor
Vox Veniae, Austin

"One of the reasons I never miss an episode of *Lost* is it makes me think. *The Gospel According to Lost* is no different. Thanks to the watchful eye of Chris Seay, the connections between this show and the deeper truths of our faith become more than interesting observations. They become a chance to consider what I believe and why. Talk about a conversation-starter!"

Greg Holder
Pastor; coauthor of *The Advent Conspiracy*; and
contributing writer for *The Voice*, a new translation of scripture

"Whenever someone can help us connect our day-to-day lives— the ones we spend, more often than not, on couches in front of the television—with the bigger, more sweeping questions of our lives (Who are we? How are we connected to one another? What matters?), there is space created for something extraordinary to happen. Chris lives in that space, and draws us into it through this book."

Shauna Niequist
Author of *Cold Tangerines*

"Chris Seay has taken one of TV's greatest shows and has brought depth, meaning, and understanding to a series that ironically prides itself on mystery. Answers will be revealed, but not necessarily the answers you were looking for. Without question, J. J. Abrams would be proud."

Mike Foster
Creative Principal at PlainJoe Studios and
author of *Deadly Viper Character Assassins*

"Within the story of *Lost*, we all find ourselves with our common expressions: love and hate, peace and fear, life and death, good and evil, truth and the unknown. Chris Seay, with his niche for the smart, the sassy, and the unconventional, leads the reader to the island—not just in the show, but the one within, where we are asked to confront and contemplate the ageless questions of mystery, the gospel, story, relationships, the Scriptures, hope, and redemption. This book does not answer all the questions *Lost* asks; in fact, it asks more. But those that get *Lost*, note that the journey is as valuable as the destination—perhaps, even more."

Mike Lawrie
Pastor, thinker, and all-around good guy

"So, just what is the gospel according to *Lost*? Chris Seay is just as mysterious and mum about the venerable TV series as the show's creators. But if you love *Lost* and have spent productive hours pondering its possibilities, Seay provides a guide for your imaginative voyage. And if you've been struck by *Lost's* biblical parallels, Seay is your surrogate castaway—along for a long and lively conversation of "What ifs" and "Yeah, buts.""

Marv Knox
Editor, Baptist Standard
Dallas, TX

"Chris has the keen eye of a missiologist who understands the windows within our culture that offer redemptive opportunities to explain the Gospel. This is another great example of his skill and insight."

Rick McKinley
Lead Pastor of Imago Dei Community
and author of *This Beautiful Mess*

"Chris Seay at the height of his powers. *The Gospel According to Lost* shows off Chris' sharp wit, thoughtful writing style and his unique ability to penetrate the Culture. Because Chris is such a fan of *Lost*, the reader is able to revel along in the joy and mystery of all the big questions, about *Lost* and life. A really fun read and yet another book by Seay that I wish I had written."

Dan Merchant
Writer/ director/ author
Lord, Save Us From Your Followers

The Gospel
According to *Lost*

The Gospel
According to *Lost*

Chris Seay

THOMAS NELSON
Since 1798

NASHVILLE   DALLAS   MEXICO CITY   RIO DE JANEIRO

This book was not authorized, prepared, approved, licensed, or endorsed by ABC and/or Disney Enterprises, Inc. or any other person or entity involved with the Lost television series. Lost is a registered trademark of Disney Enterprises, Inc., 500 South Buena Vista Street, Burbank, California.

Published in Nashville, Tennessee, by Thomas Nelson. Thomas Nelson is a registered trademark of Thomas Nelson, Inc.

Thomas Nelson, Inc., titles may be purchased in bulk for educational, business, fund-raising, or sales promotional use. For information, please e-mail SpecialMarkets@ThomasNelson.com.

Unless otherwise noted, Scripture quotations are taken from *The Voice*. © 2008 and 2009 Ecclesia Bible Society. Used by permission. All rights reserved.

Scripture quotations marked NIV are from the HOLY BIBLE: NEW INTERNATIONAL VERSION®. © 1973, 1978, 1984 by International Bible Society. Used by permission of Zondervan Publishing House. All rights reserved.

Scripture quotations marked KJV are from the KING JAMES VERSION.

Scripture quotations marked NKJV are from THE NEW KING JAMES VERSION. © 1982 by Thomas Nelson, Inc. Used by permission. All rights reserved.

Library of Congress Cataloging-in-Publication Data

Seay, Chris.
  The gospel according to Lost / Chris Seay.
     p. cm.
  Includes bibliographical references.
  ISBN 978-0-8499-2072-1 (pbk.)
  1. Lost (Television program) 2. Television broadcasting—Moral and ethical aspects. I. Title.
  PN1992.77.L67S43 2009
  791.45'72—dc22

                                                    2009039265

Printed in the United States of America

10 11 12 13 RRD 9 8 7 6 5 4 3

Tommy Head did everything to the extreme. Eleven years ago, he and his wife, Angela, gave up the life they knew to work with native tribes deep in the Amazon rain forest. His passion for life was only exceeded by his passion to bring clean water to the forgotten people of the Amazon. "If we don't serve these people," he would say, "who will?"

In 2002, Tommy and Angela started drilling wells (and teaching others to do the same), traveling hours by boat in piranha- and anaconda-infested rivers to live and work in native villages. Today, Living Water International Peru thrives through two well-trained national teams that seek to love their neighbors with clean water.

Tommy was a teacher, a hippie, a motocross king, a gifted administrator, a friend like no other, and an inspiration to everyone who met him. He found his way in the deepest, darkest jungles, and I pray that his footprints will lead those of us who are still lost in the jungle of our own selfish pursuits into the adventure of rediscovering who we can be through love and the power of God.

Table of Contents

Acknowledgments

To my family and my lovely wife, Lisa, I am so grateful for all of you and am so excited about my newest niece and nephew, David Yenenah and Sosy Seay.

Ecclesia, it is a privilege to serve you as we seek to see the gospel of our Liberating King change the world. Thank you for believing in miracles and looking for the best in other people. I love you all!

Alison Wisdom, it has been a pleasure working on this with you. Your intelligence and love for *Lost* has made this a much better book.

J. Wakeham and Kelly Hall, thanks for your contributions, editorial help, honest feedback, and great ideas.

Thanks to Dustin Hatfield, Elizabeth Puente, Robert Crowl, Daniel Park, Steven Hicks, John Starr, Wayne Brown, Houston Farris, Jack Wisdom, Gideon Tsang, Scott Erickson, Steven Hicks, RSB, and so many others who have picked up on so many things during the writing of this book.

My amazing agent, Esther Fedorkevich, I am so grateful for your partnership on this and many future projects.

Matt Baugher, it has been a joy working with you on

this unique book. I am also grateful to the entire Thomas Nelson family, namely Mike Hyatt, Tammy Heim, Frank Couch, Maleah Bell, Jennifer McNeil, and many others who work faithfully to get books and Bibles printed and available for sale in so many stores.

Rick McKinley, Greg Holder, and all the Advent Conspirators, I pray that we all continue to Worship Fully, Spend Less, Give More, and Love All!

Jay and Jack Podcast, you guys are hilarious, and I am grateful that you keep the *Lost* discussion moving forward every week. I also enjoy the many bloggers who elevate this conversation.

Ecclesia Bible Society and all the team working on *The Voice*, your hard work in bringing the Scriptures to life for those who may have never heard this good news is forever appreciated.

To Sky Bar in Galveston, your sushi was the fuel that made this project a reality. I am also grateful to others who shared good food to keep me writing, especially Pappasitos, The Houstonian, Pointe West, Taft Street Coffee, Mai's, T'Afia, Jaspers, Doyles, and Tia Maria's—thanks for allowing me to eat and write at your fine establishments.

Finally to J. J. Abrams, Carlton Cuse, Damon Lindelof, the *Lost* writers, and the amazing cast who take the time to respect their audience and tell a new story. We are all grateful!

Prologue

Television—and all of the good and bad that goes with it—defines much of who we are as a culture. Television motivates conversations and often determines, whether adversely or positively, what we value in life. We must, then, be mindful of our intake. We monitor the nutritional essentials our bodies need; we stress the importance of a balanced diet. Similarly, the public is in need of a balanced *media* diet. Much of television programming—mind-numbing talk shows, soap operas, and reality TV—should come with a disclaimer: "Warning: Watching the following program is likely to stunt one's emotional, intellectual, and spiritual growth."

Unfortunately, more than any other form of mass media, the majority of television programming has become predictable, formulaic, and generally lacking in any real spiritual or intellectual substance. The formulas that produce shows like *CSI* and laugh-out-loud sitcoms are intended to hold our attention for strategically placed advertisements. The stories here are not meant to inspire us or provoke thought. They don't intend to make the world a better place or challenge society to reach moral truths. The goal is simple: keep us on the couch as long as possible—or at least long enough to hear from one more big-money commercial.

In the entire history of television, we can point to only a few programs that were created with no regard for the dominant formulas. And when it happened, they were hallowed, happy accidents in which brilliant writers collided with mythic stories. Shows like *M*A*S*H*, *The Sopranos*, *Seinfeld*, *The Simpsons*, and *Lost* came out of nowhere, breaking the molds by attracting large numbers of participants into a story that no one imagined or expected.

Lost is not just a television show; it has become an epic story filled with mystery that has garnered twenty-three million participants. Some might call them viewers, but a participant of *Lost* doesn't sit in front of flickering electronic pixels, seeking to escape life through subpar television programming. *Lost* requires us to be involved. The story, which has blossomed into a marathon of cultural, literary, scientific, and religious allusions, offers to its faithful adherents ideas worth pondering, books worth reading, scientific theories worth exploring, and ideas that very nearly burn a hole in our pockets. *Lost*, in all its illustrative, complex glory, demands that we dialogue, research, meet ourselves in the characters, and share our latest discoveries with one another.

Lost—the story of a group of people marooned on an

island after a plane crash—has become a cultural phenomenon. The story is like an onion being peeled back week after week. As one question is answered, half a dozen new questions emerge. The questions drive us. In fact, the narrative of the show asks more questions than it answers (which either frustrates us or causes us to seek and inform ourselves). And just when we think we have it all figured out, our theory is discredited during the next episode.

What makes this series unique is not merely the distinctive flashbacks and flash-forwards through time, the infinite twists and turns of the narratives, the endless symbolism, clever and often subtle references to philosophy and theology, spellbinding storylines, and captivating mysteries. It is the sum of these parts that has created an entirely new genre of television and attracted what may be the most committed and diverse fan base in television history. College students are discussing the show with their grandmothers, professors are citing the show in their teaching, and adolescent boys are buying posters of Evangeline Lily in the same way my generation bought posters of Farrah Fawcett. Theologians engage the historical and biblical references, blue-collar workers discuss the show on their breaks, white-collar workers debate their theories around water coolers, and on an island off the coast of Honduras, kids in an orphanage raptly and faithfully follow the antics of the castaways via bootleg copies of the series. (True story.)

As with all good stories, *Lost's* success depends on our capacity to love the show's characters and identify with them—even though these island inhabitants are a collection of unlovables. Because instead of stranding an endearing crew of strangers to whom everyone can relate (for example, Gilligan, the Professor, Mary Ann, and Ginger), our castaways are composed of a surgeon with addiction problems, a murderer (and a mass murderer), a con man, a junkie, a lifelong loser, and an Iraqi soldier. It hardly sounds like a recipe for success.

Who would choose to love such outwardly broken people? Surprisingly enough, we do, and we embrace them not despite their brokenness, but often because of it. The show hits places that we all know. You may not have been stranded on an island (much less a magical island), but you know what it feels like to be lost. You might recall dreams about being adrift on a vast ocean, veering off course in a dense forest, or aimlessly wandering the streets of unfamiliar cities. We have all felt that pit in our stomachs, a deep fear, an ominous voice that unrelentingly tells us, *I am never going to survive this*. We are in need of rescue, of salvation, just as much as Sawyer and Kate.

It seems that over the last five seasons of this ABC hit series, a group of castaways, along with its followers, have experienced a veritable conversion, a turn toward something transcendent. This journey toward belief is as authentic as

Sawyer's Southern drawl, but believers in *Lost* are often approaching faith from radically different perspectives. Jack believes only what he can see and tangibly confirm, but Locke has discovered faith while blindly but hopefully groping through his experiences and learning to trust his intuition. Unlikely as it seems, it is possible that this epic television series may be filled with stories that inspire us to love both God and one another, wisdom that will lead us toward a vibrant relationship with God, and insights into a life of true faith.

In the midst of all of its action, mystery, suspense, and romance, *Lost* is a story filled with substance. The focus on faith and truth is never more clearly explained than in the words of John Locke as he questions Jack Shephard. "Why do you find it so hard to believe?" Locke asks. Jack shoots back, "Why do you find it so easy?" Locke then patiently and succinctly sums up his faith, explaining, "It's never been easy." This tension between faith and reason is what drives the story line. Locke adds insight as he explains to Jack, "You and I don't see eye to eye sometimes because you're a man of science. Me, well, I'm a man of faith."[1]

Being on this island has changed Jack. This man of science now speaks of destiny and faith. He seems to have redefined his worldview, shifted his own paradigm, and found—or is seeking—a new way to live. And the show can change our ideas too. *The Gospel According to* Lost is an exploration of the seemingly infinite ideas, philosophies, scientific observations, and biblical metaphors that make the *Lost* story are more than engaging, but educational. It is an invitation to dive deep into a fascinating narrative, to be suspended upon a web that weaves in truth from Flannery O'Connor, quantum physics, and the Enlightenment, as well as postmodern philosophy, ancient mystics, and the Bible.

If *Lost* manages to get millions of people exploring these ideas and truly wrestling with them, then it has accomplished what no television series has dared to dream before. As John Locke explains to Charlie, as they gaze upon a small-blanketed creature, "This moth's just about to emerge. It's in there right now, struggling. It's digging its way through the thick hide of the cocoon. Now, I could help it—take my knife, gently widen the opening, and the moth would be free—but it would be too weak to survive. Struggle is nature's way of strengthening it." May the blessing of this book be that we struggle well together—and in the end find that we emerge from these pages stronger.

Embracing the Mystery

Mystery is a resource, like coal or gold,
and its preservation is a fine thing.

—Tim Cahill, American travel writer

What if I told you that I planned to answer all of your questions about *Lost* over the next 189 pages? Would you keep reading?

Inquiring minds want to know: What is that island? Will Sawyer hook up with Kate? How did the women on this island end up with only tank tops to wear? Is Jacob a man or God—or something in between? Is Sayid dead or alive—and if he recovers, who will he shoot next? Is *what happened, happened* always true? If Desmond calls all men "brutha" in conversation, what does he say when speaking to a woman—"sistah"? Are the good guys always good, and are bad guys bad through and through, or is there a sliding scale of morality? What's with the Others' tendency to speak so inopportunely in Latin? Is Richard Alpert related to Dick Clark? (He never ages, and, after all, they do share the same first name.) Some of us watch *Lost* because we just have to know the answers—and we want them now.

If you are hoping this is a book filled with spoilers that explain it all . . . I am sorry, but you have purchased the wrong book. And I apologize, but I won't give you your money back—not in this economy. Do not misunderstand me; I also want to know the answers. It is true that the questions drive me, but the sense of wonder that comes with not knowing is what has me intellectually invested in this story. For the 246 or so days between seasons five and six, the mysteries raised in the final minutes of that last episode of season five will bombard my brain with a slew of questions: What kind of loophole was needed to kill Jacob? Is the man seeking to kill him—cloaked in the form of John Locke— his brother Esau? This answer, when it comes (and I do believe this is one of the questions that will be answered), will help in assembling the puzzled pieces of this narrative. But it is unlikely the answer will satisfy me. In fact, as one well versed in the history and conflict of Jacob and Esau, I stand a strong chance of being disappointed. Not to knock the talented writers who create this show, but the scenarios I have developed in my mind might be better than what they ultimately present on the screen. Budgets, sets, actors, contracts, or special effects do not limit my imagination, so it makes sense that my story would be superior. As much as I value the answers—or the truth, if you will—it is often the journey to find truth that shapes me more than the revelation of the truth itself.

The purpose of this book is not to erase the mystery, but to allow each of us to seek a posture that celebrates the things we do know and to embrace the mystery of things that have yet to unfold. We may find that the unknown is more valuable, meaningful, and useful in stimulating the imagination than the known. Albert Einstein described the link between mystery and intelligence this way: "The most beautiful thing we can experience is the mysterious. It is the source of all true art and science. He to whom this emotion is a stranger, who can no longer pause to wonder and stand rapt in awe, is as good as dead: his eyes are closed."[1] If you have remained a participant of *Lost* beyond season one, you are likely someone who enjoys this pursuit and has learned to seek true art and science as you rummage through the story line of your favorite show.

In order to appreciate the connection this narrative has with mystery, one must delve into the mind of *Lost* cocreator J. J. Abrams. It may be that his disciplined pursuit of mystery has nurtured the imaginative intelligence it takes to bring to life ingenious series like *Lost* and *Alias*, or to revive an ailing franchise like *Star Trek*. Abrams's love for the unknown is hardly a storytelling fad; it is a lifelong pursuit. As a child, Abrams would go to a quirky magic shop in midtown Manhattan with his beloved grandfather, who once bought him a Tannen's Magic Mystery Box filled with fifty dollars' worth of magic tricks. This striking box filled with surprises is the ultimate treasure for an aspiring young magician and storyteller, but young Abrams chose to not open the box—in fact, he still has not opened it.

The mysterious box marked only with a question mark sits on a shelf next to his desk, and he continues to wonder about the infinite possibilities of what the box contains. Abrams says, "It represents hope. It represents potential. Mystery boxes are everywhere in what I do. That blank page is a magic box. What are stories but mystery boxes?"[2] He has a point. Every time a storyteller intentionally withholds information, he creates a mystery box, while his audience waits patiently to learn more about the characters and the plot into which we have been drawn.

If mystery heightens the experience of the story, then why do some people ruin it for themselves and others by reading the last page of a novel, or hitting spoiler Web sites before the big finale? Abrams himself points out in the March 2009 issue of *Wired* magazine that the word *spoil* means to ruin or damage irreparably. A story experienced without the unknown would be damaged, but we sometimes fail to patiently page through novels to let stories unfold in their own time because ultimately we are creatures who crave the safety of knowing what is going to happen, the comfort of a mystery resolved. We were created from mystery to live in mystery—to trek an adventure of faith—but instead of embracing the process, we stir and squirm until we find an answer to anchor us, to make us feel safe. Can you imagine walking through life with a foreknowledge of every second of the day? You may think that we as a society groan enough now over the mundane, but just picture, for a moment, knowing the outcome of everything. The unknown is a gift, one that in its universality still retains its novelty. It is always relevant, always significant. We were made to walk in this way together. Our eyes are not meant to see what lies in every shadowed corner, but to blindly, faithfully, and thrillingly take steps toward an unforeseen ending. And, as the survivors of Oceanic Flight 815 discover, it is often in the shadows that we find our answers.

Why do people seek out spoilers? Some just enjoy the opportunity to extol themselves as the first to know. They basically want to bandage their insecurity; they want you to know how much better they are because they know (and how they are superior to you because you *aren't* in the know). For a moment it may feel good to have the answers and let the uninformed recognize our higher intellect. But those of us who choose to sit with mystery hope our patient journey will form our character in constructive ways. The seductive belief that we have decoded and solved the puzzle, that we have finally arrived and found all the answers, gives birth to an arrogance that repulses even our most devoted supporters. So we must beware; the pursuit of answers, or quest for truth, will keep us humble.

What we are most likely to discover in the end is that the most important questions to answer are not about what the island is, or the true identity of Jacob. It is our willing-ness to ask deeper, life-altering questions that impact who we are and how we treat one another that truly matters. Frederick Buechner best explains the way a mystery calls out those willing to embark on a true spiritual quest as he explores the power of the unknown: "Religion points to that area of human experience where in one way or another man comes upon mystery as a summons to pilgrimage."[3] It is possible that the questions that naturally arise in this plot will beckon you to study, read, meditate, pray, discuss, debate, and become informed in ways that will change you, as together we ask:

- When is violence justifiable? Is torture ever an acceptable treatment of another human being?
- Does love ultimately lead to self-sacrifice, or are we all on a journey of self-preservation?
- Is morality black and white, or are there shades of gray?
- Is our destiny irrevocably mapped out, or do we have the ability to craft our own purpose?
- Does free will truly exist?
- Can people change?

If you are like me, you are often confronted with the reality that you have not yet become the person you want to be. Let us hope—and not just for the sake of Kate, Jack, and Sawyer—that people really can change. May we all know and experience the change that can only come by embracing the great mysteries of this universe and walking humbly in that embrace. May we open our eyes and awake from our slumber; as Annie Dillard says in *Pilgrim at Tinker Creek*, her classic book of essays, "We wake, if we ever wake at all, to mystery."[4]

Life as Backgammon

All things truly wicked start from an innocence.

—Ernest Hemingway (*A Moveable Feast*, 1964)

Lost is a complex story. Each plot, each story line, is infused with deeper meaning. Leadership effortlessly transforms into control, love into jealousy, empathy into rage, and hope is at one moment near and at another drifting farther away on a tide of uncertainty. It is easy to get caught up in a particular narrative and believe for a time that *Lost* is about physical, human tension: we watch Jack and Locke butt heads; we want to strangle Kate as she bounces back and forth between Sawyer and Jack; we try to make heads or tails out of the relationships between Jacob and the unnamed Man in Black, and Ben Linus and Charles Widmore. Yes, it's easy to look at *Lost* as simply a good example of the most primal human conflicts, but doing so undermines the essence of the show. Ultimately it is about good versus evil, black and white, the Creator and the Adversary. In episode two of the first season, John Locke inadvertently (okay, maybe the writers knew what they were doing) but accurately identifies the true conflict while explaining to Walt the rules, oddly enough, of backgammon; there are, he says, "two players, two sides; one is light, one is dark."

Essentially *Lost* is a story about the struggle between good and evil, expressed in a rather far-fetched and fantastical way, much like Tolkien's Lord of the Rings trilogy or C. S. Lewis's Chronicles of Narnia stories. All epic stories are based on this battle to see everything good and right prevail over evil and corruption; it's a literary archetype. This struggle is not a hook inserted into the *Lost* narrative to keep viewers in their seats through a commercial break; it lies at the core of the story, and apparently goes back to the beginning. In the sixth episode of the series, the Losties find two skeletons, who become known as Adam and Eve. Jack finds in possession of one of the skeletons a small bag that contains two rocks, one black and the other white. The island is the stage for this epic battle, but unlike the mystical land of Narnia, the inhabitants of this island often combat evil in all the wrong ways. Sophocles said, "All concerns of men go wrong when they wish to cure evil with evil,"[1] and this is a lesson the Losties have thus far failed to learn. As each character fights for what he or she perceives as good and right, the lines are blurred, and at times it seems as though the character is swallowed by darkness himself. Friedrich Nietzsche aptly described this power of evil in a book he called *Beyond Good and Evil*, saying, "Whoever fights monsters should see to it that in the process he does not become a monster. And when you look long into an abyss, the abyss also looks into you."[2]

But it is also true, as Joseph Campbell says, that we find our greatest treasures as we delve into the abyss. Our hope is that the characters we have grown to love will be redeemed by this journey, not corrupted by it.

This tension makes *Lost* different from other epic stories such as Narnia, Star Wars, or Lord of the Rings: we are never exactly sure who is good and who is evil. In Tolkien's books, we know to always root for hobbits; and in Lewis's, we know we should never trust anyone who is responsible for making it winter but never Christmas. But with *Lost*, we find ourselves debating our loyalties. Sure, we are likely to remain faithful to the original Losties, but what about Ben? Widmore? Jacob? The writers know what they're doing. They know they're toying with our trust, and we simultaneously love them and hate them for it; the entire series is littered with clues that hint to the difficulty of ambiguity. For example, Ben's face is oftentimes depicted halfway covered in shadows, while the other half remains in the light. It hardly takes a genius to deduce, *Aha! This is to remind the audience that we* still *don't know whether or not to trust Ben.* Similarly, remember how strange Locke seemed at the beginning of the show? We weren't exactly sure if he was good, bad, or just a little odd . . . and as if to confirm that, in the first-season episode "Raised by Another," Claire has a dream in which Locke appears with one black eye and one white eye. And what about Sawyer? When Sayid makes him glasses to cure his headaches, we see that the glasses are composed of two frames fused together: one black, the other white. Back then we weren't sure of Sawyer's character either, and this little detail reflected that uncertainty. In other words, it's in the nature of the show to keep us guessing. It's annoying at times, but at least when we find out the truth—the real, honest-to-Jacob truth—we staunchly adhere to it. It means that much more because of the struggle it took to put all the pieces together. And isn't this, more than anything else in the show, reflective of our everyday, magic-islandless lives? Think about this in terms of spirituality. John Calvin stood by the theory of a *sensus divinitatis*, or an innate sense of the divine; he asserted that we all were born with a universal tendency toward belief. We were created to believe. This is a powerful sentiment, and while it cannot necessarily be proven, most Christians will resonate with it, at least theoretically. But, of course, no life is without ambiguity or confusion. There's the problem of evil in the world, and while our problem may be not with God but with the world he's created, it's still a major problem in our faith. Reader, be warned: this chapter isn't going to attempt to solve this dilemma; this non sequitur is offered only to reiterate the idea that when we suffer, when we confront the big problems of who and what is truly good, we grow. And when we finally move out of those shadowy places, the ground seems to be a bit more firm.

All the evidence in *Lost* is pointing to the existence of a truly good higher power; and, in turn, to the existence of evil. We know that the core of the show is, like our lives, a struggle between these two interfaces, and how this struggle manifests itself in every facet of these complex scenarios. We see it in the ways the Losties relate to one another. We see it in the ways the Losties interact with the Others. We see it reflected in how they engage and entertain the idea of a providential being. The show uses this concept of duality to communicate the idea of epic and personal struggle—the struggle that pits us against each other, against God, and even against what lies deep within ourselves. Ultimately, this may be what it is about *Lost* that rings particularly true—we are all filled with good and evil, our motives are mixed, and a battle is being waged within each of us on a daily basis. Even Paul the apostle suffered this inner war of wills and describes it in bare honesty in his letter to Rome, saying, "*Listen*, I can't explain my actions. Here's why: I am not able to do the things I want; and at the same time, I do the things I despise. If I am doing the things I have already decided not to do, I am agreeing with the law regarding what is good. But now I am no longer the one acting—I've lost control—sin has taken up residence in me and is wreaking havoc. I know that in me, that is, in my fallen human nature, there is nothing good. I can will myself to do something good, but that does not help me to carry it out. I can determine that I am going to do good, but I don't do it; instead, I end up living out the evil that I decided not to do" (Romans 7:15–19). It sounds as if these words could have been uttered by any of our castaways, who seem to universally believe that they are losing the inner battle and have moved beyond the pale of redemption. But the *Lost* narrative is uniquely intertwined with the Judeo-Christian story, and the beauty of Christianity is found in its unyielding proclamation that no one is beyond redemption—not even a torturer, murderer, or con man.

Numbers Don't Lie—Hurley:
Patron Saint of Blessed Losers

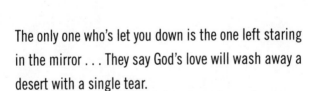

The only one who's let you down is the one left staring in the mirror . . . They say God's love will wash away a desert with a single tear.

—Bill Mallonee, American singer-songwriter

There is little debate that the island heals physical brokenness: it miraculously cured Locke's paralysis and sent Rose's cancer into permanent remission. But with Hurley, we see that the island can also heal emotional brokenness. Hugo "Hurley" Reyes may be the quintessential American loser. His dad abandons him as a young boy, and he copes with the loss by eating everything he can get his hands on, especially chicken. So to gain access to his drug of choice (fried poultry) he takes a job at the perennially greasy Mr. Cluck's Chicken Shack, and, as we all well know, nothing says "stuck in a rut" like employment at a fast-food place. Even his own mother finds his life mildly abhorrent, and she lectures him on his laziness: "The only time you move is to lift a drumstick out of the bucket. Every day is the same thing, Hugo: work, TV, chicken. You have to change your life, Hugo. You think someone else will do it for you? Maybe if you pray every day, Jesus Christ will come down from heaven, take two hundred pounds, and bring you a decent woman and a new car. Yes—Jesus can bring you a new car!" The message is clear: even with a new car, the only woman who will love you is your mother, and even she seems to be at her breaking point.

One could argue that Hurley's actions hurt no one but himself. Well, except for that time Hurley's four-hundred-pound girth became the straw that broke the residential deck, killing four unsuspecting people partying below. This guilt is more than he can bear, and he believes he has committed obesity manslaughter. Ultimately his inability to cope lands him in Santa Rosa Mental Health facility, where he plays Connect Four with an imaginary friend and listens to a fellow patient named Leonard repeat the same strange set of numbers over and over. Upon his release, Hurley plays those numbers—4, 8, 15, 16, 23, 42—in the lottery and wins $114 million. Problem solved, right? Sadly, it is not that easy for Hurley. As his mother lovingly reminds him, even a new car cannot get him a decent woman, and if he had trouble finding a true friend when he was a broke loser, imagine how difficult it will be as a millionaire.

Hurley can finally buy whatever his heart desires: a Hummer, Mr. Cluck's Chicken Shack, a home for his mother, video games, a home theater . . . everything except what he truly wants: a father and a real friend. The island brings him the friendships he never knew before—and as far as a father figure goes, well, maybe Jacob will be a father to all of these fatherless castaways. Or could it be that the new Hurley heals emotionally when his father returns and begins to pursue him, even giving him the classic, fully restored Camaro they used to work on together when Hugo was a child?

Hurley the couch potato is transformed after the crash—from a textbook loser to the island's activity coordinator. He is inspired to design a golf course, repair a Dharma bus for a legendary joy ride, and entertain his fellow castaways with a refreshing sense of humor that endears him to each and every person on the island. The obese teddy bear whom Sawyer calls "Jabba" and sometimes "Deep Dish" is, without a doubt, the most beloved person on the island.

Damon Lindelof, the cocreator of *Lost*, says Hurley is the most morally grounded of all the characters on this show. Despite the fact that Michael kills the only woman he has ever loved, Hurley chooses to not seek retribution and manages to find peace through his pain. He knows the difference between right and wrong, and he is physically incapable of lying about Oceanic 815. The charade put forward by Jack and the Oceanic 6 devastates him. His core values are truth and loyalty, yet he is asked to either lie or betray his friends and, operating on his moral code, either way he loses. In the strain of this conflict, he is surrendering slowly to madness.

Did a curse bring his plane crashing onto a deserted

island, or was it a blessing? On the island Hurley finds friends who seem to truly love him for who he is, and he even finds love (although tragically fleeting), reciprocated by the sweet and pretty Libby. As Sayid believes he is beyond the reach of salvation, Hurley echoes that sentiment when he screams at Libby, "Look, you can't help me! No one can." He constantly reminds himself that the curse not only exists, but also prevails. His unswerving loyalty to predetermination paralyzes Hurley, and he resigns himself to wriggling under a curse rather than struggling to embrace a blessing. Jacob sees it differently, however, and our patron saint of losers may be more blessed than anyone in his family or on the island, if he only had eyes to see the blessings instead of the curses.

Our distinctly human freedom to choose is an essential part of the *Lost* gospel. If Jacob has a brief window in time to get one point across, it seems that ten times out of ten, that message will be, "You have a choice." We possess the ability to choose our path even if that path turns dark and twisted and leads us directly into Smokey's lair or into the ambiguously dangerous clutches of the Others. We author our own adventures: leave the island, pierce Jacob with a serrated dagger, buy a lottery ticket, kill your abusive stepfather/actual father, rescue a twelve-year-old who is destined to become a mass murderer, push the button . . . or don't. You may live to regret it, but your choice it will remain. After all, to paraphrase Daniel Faraday, what happened, happened.

Despite this power to choose, this gift of freedom, it seems that much of the world is uncertain, chaotic, and evidently out of control. There are forces at work much larger than the decisions we make, and these powers seem able to create dark clouds or sunshine with an apparently divine will. Hurley believes that the cosmic force designed to compel him into a life of misery is a shadowy curse—or perhaps his fate is even determined by multiple curses.

At first, Hurley seems like a superstitious fool to subscribe to such an antiquated belief system. "Really, Hurley?" we ask the TV. "You are cursed? Who believes in curses anymore?" We remind ourselves that words do not have power; we convince ourselves that words disappear in the air as quickly as we speak them. Ancient peoples believed that kind of mysterious nonsense, but surely we are above that. Our world is one of science and facts, not a world governed by utterances of blind faith and inane ignorance. We cannot in good conscience inhabit the latter world . . . or can we?

In the Bible, curses and blessings are often traced back

to the father. Isaac, the blessed son of Abraham, was expected to bless one of his own sons soon after the death of his father. His sons witnessed the power of blessings and curses as their father, Isaac, was reunited with their uncle, Ishmael, to bury their grandfather, Abraham. It must have been clear to both sons that the favored and blessed son was sure to experience the wealth, fame, and plentiful life that was destined to elude the other. In the end, Isaac had won his father's affection, wealth, substantial estate, and the confidence that he was, in short, special, called to something magnificent like his father. On the other hand, Ishmael got a trip as a young infant into the desert with a single bottle of water. Were Jacob and Esau at Abraham's funeral? Were they born yet? According to the Talmud, their pursuit of their father's blessing began in the days after Abraham's death.

What might someone in Ishmael's position have been willing to do to gain the upper hand? We can be assured that Jacob and Esau were watching all of this carefully, and watching quickly turned to plotting. As the brothers returned home to enter a time of mourning, it must have been clear that the favored son who received both the birthright of the inheritance and a blessing from their father would have the chance to pursue his dreams, while the other would struggle to carve out a meager existence. What might they have been willing to do to gain the upper hand?

This pursuit of a blessing was not just a dilemma for these ancient brothers; it hangs like a dark cloud over many prestigious and successful people I know. Many prominent artists and businesspeople push themselves to dizzying heights, unsatisfied even by grand accomplishments; they seek spoken approval long into adulthood. They strive at all costs to hear a blessing or kind word from a parent or mentor—words that are often never uttered, thus their absence is always gnawing.

Hurley's belief system, primarily how he regards his own destiny and existence, is similarly determined by his paternal relationship. One of the most beautiful parts of *Lost* is the attention paid to the shaping of personalities and development of individual modi operandi. Hurley, perhaps more than any other character, struggles with both accepting and relinquishing control of his life, and through a poignant (albeit sad) conversation with his father, we see the root of Hurley's struggle. David Reyes tells his young son, "Having hope is never stupid. You gotta believe good things will happen; then they will. In this world, son, you've gotta make your own luck." With this advice dispensed and a comforting candy bar offered, David Reyes hops on his motorcycle to test his philosophy in Vegas. Then over the next seventeen years, he does not utter another word or even send a clichéd birthday greeting to his young son.

It seems that Hurley's dad has read some Norman Vincent Peale, and while the power of positive thinking maintains merit in some circumstances, here we see the difficulty of translating this mantra into actuality. It is no wonder, then, that a young boy attempts to believe himself into a desirable future but ultimately cannot overcome the reality that his father walked out of his life for seventeen years. Doing so just moments after uttering those fateful (no pun intended) words leaves the young Hugo a casualty of the acerbic backlash of poorly dispensed advice. He is not alone in this abandonment: these events in Hurley's life echo his biblical predecessor, who was discarded in the desert with only a bottle of water. Ishmael's life also unfolds according to the will of his earthly father. So where does that leave us? How malleable are our lives in the hands of those around us? Can these actions mold our fates? Do our destinies depend on the kindness or enmity of others?

Hurley's dad shapes his son even in his absence. He is largely responsible for who his son grows up to be: overweight, slightly disillusioned, someone who blames his troubles on a force that he cannot recognize, much less prove its existence.

Words have power. They possess a mystical quality that is difficult to quantify or define. In recent years, a Japanese researcher, Masaru Emoto, has been embraced by many and scorned by others for his controversial research on the power of intentions. In a quest to determine the power words possess, he attempted to measure the effects in simple tests on two base and primal elements: rice and water. The rice bowl experiment has been reproduced countless times in homes, classrooms, coffee shops, and community centers; and it can be seen repeatedly on YouTube, which, as we know, is the litmus test for cultural significance. In this simple experiment, which I first witnessed in my child's kindergarten classroom, two jars of cooked rice are observed; one jar is given a blessing, and the other a curse. One jar bears the words *thank you*, and the other simply the word *fool*; the blessing and curse is then reinforced verbally over a period of time. Emoto, as well as many other participants, claims that the "blessed" jar of rice ages gently as it ferments, but the "cursed" jar quickly spoils, becoming rotten and putrid. The experiment in my child's classroom produced the same results.

One may question the science practiced in such unorthodox laboratories, or ridicule an experiment that gained its notoriety on the Internet instead of in scientific journals. This idea, however, is very consistent with the Hebrew worldview embodied by Abraham, Isaac, and Jacob in the biblical narrative—words possess power, whether they are names given to children, curses spoken to enemies, blessings offered to our loved ones, or even haphazard advice extended in the hurried moments before departure.

You have likely even felt physical effects from spoken words: butterflies flit about your stomach as you listen to soft whispers in the tenderness and safety of intimacy; your cheeks flush at the manifestations of anger drawn from pithy annoyances; your muscles tighten as a reckless driver sends you a message via sign language on a crowded interstate. So much lies in our communication with one another—even the most fleeting and careless of insults can wound us, so you can imagine that if you feel a physical response to a passing curse from a stranger on the highway, pronouncements of failure and worthlessness from a parent or loved one will strike sharply deep within you. It is in this way, then, that Hurley has been cursed, not by a cryptic incantation of numbers, but by imprudent words.

Similarly, Charlie cannot shake the dire prediction of the Scots hatch dweller: "Desmond says I am going to die." In fact we will all die, but Desmond's prophecy seems more ominous. He says, "No matter what, Charlie, you're going to die." So Charlie mopes around because he believes Desmond's words. He keeps living on the island, but not in the way he had before. He waits—believing that death lurks around every corner. Finally, at the end of his life,

Charlie is resigned to his fate, and even ready for it when the time arrives. But did Charlie choose his path and accept his destiny or decide to believe a curse?

What if Isaac and Abraham were only half right? What if they understood the power of blessings and curses but struggled with an inaccurate view of our human capacity for love and blessings? Often in our emotional, spiritual, and financial economy, the problem is that we adopt a view of scarcity rather than abundance. We fear we will not have enough money, insight, or even love to share with others. As every parent experiences in the anticipation of a second child, we often doubt we could ever have the kind of love for the second child that we have for our first. But something magical happens when that child is born, when we stare into the eyes of our newborn as it clings to our chest: we grow a new heart. Our capacity for love doubles, and sometimes triples. Isaac, like his father before him, allowed a blessing on one son to become a curse to the other. As the Scriptures say and the Others may be reminded often: "Jacob I loved, but Esau I hated" (Romans 9:13 NIV). It is clear that young Hugo's earthly father could not even find the time to send an annual birthday card, but his ultimate healing may be more dramatic than Locke emerging from a wheelchair.

Jacob plotted, with the help of his mother, to steal both the birthright and the blessing from his brother,

Esau. As Esau stood famished, he traded his birthright for a pot of Hebrew chowder. The blessing heist became even more complicated; it required costumes, fake hair, and the like. But in the end, Jacob heard his father bless him, and ultimately those words became Jacob's reality. Did the blessing help him walk the right path? Did it destine his future actions? In life, as in *Lost*, we may never be sure. But one thing is certain: as Brazilian writer Paulo Coelho has said, "A blessing ignored will become a curse."[1] May we choose to bless others at every opportunity and see the blessings that encircle our paths, that either destine or assist us in finding our contented future.

Sayid Jarrah: Patron Saint
of Tormented Humanitarians

One's real life is often the life that one does not lead.

—Oscar Wilde, Irish author (1854–1900)

Death, pain, and suffering are realities in this world. But many of us live with blinders on, our eyes strategically directed elsewhere. We prefer to ignore the cruelties of war, the devastation and disease caused by poverty, or the truth about human nature. So to ensure we continue living in a blissful state of unawareness, we make sure that our news sources are sanitized, our novels are uplifting, and that the chicken breast we grill for dinner comes neatly packaged from the store. But behind all the Cling Wrap is a story, a story that does not have easy answers or simple moral mandates.

As a young boy, Sayid was willing to embrace the realities that others chose to ignore. His father, attempting to make a man out of Sayid's older brother, demands that he kill the family chicken. His brother stands paralyzed before the small creature, incapable of taking the life of this innocent fowl; but at four years of age, Sayid unflinchingly steps forward and kills the chicken that would feed his family that evening. On the island, the general populous, including Benjamin Linus, declare Sayid a born killer. He is capable of inflicting pain to extract truth, pulling the trigger to execute a woman or child, and he does it all without the slightest hesitation. Is he a monster? This, of course, is hard to say; after all, on *Lost*, nothing is what it appears to be. One moment he is executing someone's father on a golf course, and the next he is building homes for the poor in the Dominican Republic. Is he evil? Yes. Does he love? Yes. Is he beyond the pale of redemption? He believes himself to be past the point of transformation, but I have a feeling that Jacob may disagree.

In an effortless examination, the problems of the world can be blamed on men like Sayid. On the surface he is a cold-blooded killer, and he easily becomes who our instinctual reactions allow him to be. As he prepares to board Oceanic 815, he asks Shannon, a fellow passenger, to watch his bag momentarily. She looks but does not see, allowing herself only time to register dark skin and Middle Eastern features. To Shannon, Sayid could not possibly be in Australia cooperating with the CIA to foil a terrorist plot, and exists only as a threat to her security; accordingly she turns him over to airport security, which releases him just in time to board the flight.

Is Sayid guilty? Undoubtedly, Sayid is plagued by his culpability. But, like all of us, Sayid can hardly be defined by his guilt, and he embodies more than just simple destruction. After all, can we even establish the quantification of guilt? Take the chicken incident. Sayid kills the chicken not only to prove his readiness for maturity but also to feed his family. Can we really say that Sayid, because he served as the means of execution, is more responsible for the chicken's death than his hungry family? On a more profound level, is Sayid the torturer more or less guilty than soldiers or insurrecting rebels who require his services? Is it the need or action we blame? I would contend that Sayid is not necessarily more culpable than others involved in either event. We are all dining at the same table, fighting the same war. We have the same heart. We make choices based on our convenience rather than justice. Judgment awaits the innocent and the guilty—and most of us who float between the two extremes.

Chris Carabott, a video games executive, describes the island's lone Arab castaway as "a badass who could give Jack Bauer, James Bond, and Jason Bourne all a run for their money."[1] He is a soldier from Iraq with special training that allows him to remain calm amid fierce carnage. He is menacing; his ability to torture or kill without any visible tension is disquieting. Morally, I am outraged by his predisposition toward violence as the answer to all conflict. But would I want Sayid in my crew if I were stranded on an island surrounded by hostile forces? Without hesitation, but with more than a little discomfort, my answer is a resounding yes. And, to be perfectly honest, I think most of you out there, even the staunch advocates of nonviolent resistance, would be hard-pressed to argue.

So what does that say about us and how we approach the use of physical force? When we're threatened, we—without even a moment of thought—want a mercenary on our side; then, if things should go wrong, we can place any blame squarely on the shoulders of the man doing the brunt of the work, and we can continue on with our dinner parties and white picket fences, narrowly escaping the unpleasant side effects of guilt. But we all have to serve someone, and the Sayids of the world serve our society. So we must ask ourselves: What does this say about how we should treat this notion of violence, in and of itself a hotbed of controversy? Where does violence fit in with the gospel? Can it have a place in Christianity? It is, without a doubt, a difficult topic to broach—but perhaps one of the most pressing matters to resolve for modern-day Christians.

In season one Shannon has an intense asthma attack, but her inhalers are nowhere to be found. Convinced that Sawyer must have them in his possession, Sayid (prompted by Jack and his supporters) tortures Sawyer to determine where he has hidden them. After all, what's a little pain compared to saving someone's life? But here we have the dark side—the worst-case scenario—of this theory: what if we make a mistake? In the end, Sawyer does not have the inhalers but suffers anyway. This mistake, although not exactly tragic in the grand scheme of things on the island, reminds Sayid of his fallen nature. He chastises himself for his brutality and his readiness to engage in rash violence. With one of the most profound but succinct pronouncements in the entire series, Sayid identifies something tragic not only in himself but in all mankind: "There are," he says, "worse things to fear than what's in the jungle." Yes, the perils in the jungle houses are many, but they are, for the most part, conquerable. What is truly frightening is the darkness within every man and its potential manifestations. This is harder—and scarier—to pinpoint, and thus a greater challenge to overcome.

One of the most beautiful Sayid-centric episodes develops this in a heartfelt, authentic way. Sayid is taken hostage by the husband of a woman who claims Sayid tortured her in Iraq; she has the scars and the anger to prove it. She confronts Sayid after he has been beaten by her heartbroken and irate husband, and tells him a story about her life after the Iraqi prison: She moved to an apartment where she secluded herself, unable to move past what had happened to her, until one day she saw a group of kids trap a cat in a box and then throw lit firecrackers into the box. Struck by the cries of the tormented animal, she rushed outside, saved the cat, and adopted it into her home. "We are all capable of doing what those children did to that cat," she tells Sayid. "But I will not do that. I will not be that." And so she lets Sayid go.

We all have this inherent ability to hurt one another. It is distinctly human and absolutely tragic. When I imagine being stranded on an island and attacked by hostile forces, my instincts tell me that I want Sayid on my team. But is my own survival worth allowing someone else to be tortured? Is it ever justified to use or encourage brutality to protect my life? If I survive but am complicit in brutality, is that the kind of life I am willing to live? Like Sawyer, I might have second thoughts when I am the one being tortured. There would be very few supporters of waterboarding if they thought there was a chance that their turn to be strapped down was coming.

Sayid battles his capacity for evil throughout the entire series; he has seen what lies inside himself, and he is tormented by it. He cannot believe himself to be a good man because he understands the potential for destruction, and he allows himself to be undermined by it. It is this—not the potential, not his past, but his surrender—that is the great tragedy of Sayid's life. He believes himself to be past the point of redemption; the arm of change cannot reach far enough to touch him. His abhorrence of himself and his guilt prevent him from accepting the possibility of change, and so when we catch up with Sayid in season five, he is working for charity in an attempt to atone for his mistakes.

Although Jesus explicitly directs us to exchange violence and the struggle to dominate others for grace, our natural tendencies take over, and we find ourselves trying to justify our actions. When we recognize this, it hardens us or defeats us, and the idea of grace seems to become less clear. Our redemption seems less tangible, and we begin to think that through our human efforts, we can achieve it. Maybe if we trade in our gun for a hammer and set off to build a school for some orphans, we can save ourselves. But this cannot be. We cannot save ourselves. We are, through our sin, enemies of God, and it is only through the Cross, that destroyer of social paradigms, that we are reconciled . . . and this is the beauty of the gospel. We can't earn grace; God gives it to us. No one is beyond redemption. Not even Sayid.

Kate Austen: Patron Saint of Beautiful Killers

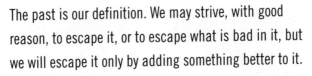

The past is our definition. We may strive, with good reason, to escape it, or to escape what is bad in it, but we will escape it only by adding something better to it.

—Wendell Berry, American writer and academic

If Hurley is the most beloved castaway on this island, Kate takes a close second, and is without a doubt the most sought after. Locke, Sawyer, and Jack seem to be fighting for preeminence as leader of the Oceanic tribe, but a true leader is the one whom people choose to follow—and that choice often depends on the will of one stunningly beautiful woman.

Kate quickly becomes a part of the island's A-team; and while she may not be fighting to lead the troops, she holds a good bit of influence over how things run. People long to be in her company, and can you blame them? Married men, myself included, must be careful how we speak of Kate in front of our wives, lest they sense our true feelings for her. Have you fallen for this small-screen temptress, previously unknown before portraying the lunch box–stealing, bank-robbing, murderous beauty we've learned to love? While Kate certainly makes cast-away chic look good, her perfect looks can't really atone for her dark history. So how could educated people fix-ate on such a character? I have no idea, but I love her still, and so do Sawyer and Jack. If the truth were told,

Locke, Ben, Hurley, and even young Walt are all praying that Kate will play Eve to their Adam. She is the essence of feminine beauty, combined with a strength that says, "If you beat my mom, I won't just kick your ass; I will kill you!" And nothing says "starlet" more than putting a man to bed, taking off his boots, turning on the gas, and lighting a match . . . then driving away on your motorcycle and never looking back as your childhood home (and father) are enveloped in flames. Certainly Kate herself is explosive, her personality combining the combustive elements of adventure, restlessness, and her own peculiar ethics. Claire, the island's resident astrologist, pinpoints Kate right away as a Gemini: "restless, passionate," a complex spirit divided against herself. But the most accurate depiction of Kate is found in lyrics penned by Bruce Springsteen, used as the title of a Kate-centric episode in season one: "Born to Run."

And run she does. From her childhood to the crash, Kate is constantly on the lam, whether physically or emotionally. It pains her to run, but the hurt that leaving brings is nothing compared to the strain of simply staying put. Long before Flight 815, Kate lived in Iowa with her mother, Diane, and her abusive stepfather—no, wait, her biological father—Wayne. Despite her mother's claims to love Wayne, Kate, easily affected by a sense of justice, devises a plan to rid them of Wayne's abuses once and for all: as mentioned earlier, Kate puts the drunken Wayne to bed and blows up the house. She confesses her involvement to her mother, who, appalled by her daughter's actions and racked by an inexplicable but authentic sadness, calls the authorities on Kate. Betrayed by her mother, Kate begins an odyssey of deception while on the run from the same U.S. marshal we see die in season one. Over the three years of fleeing her fate, Kate experiences more heartbreak: she marries and runs away; she is rejected by her mother and runs away; she watches her childhood best friend die and runs away; she struggles with her complicity in his accidental death . . . and she runs away. The marshal finally apprehends her in Australia, and together they board Oceanic 815, which, of course, crashes on the island, allowing Kate to escape her past once again.

The island has a way of recognizing each castaway's Achilles' heel and bringing about a healing journey as each confronts his or her weaknesses. Where can she run on an island? There is no diversion from reality, no escape from her problems. Kate has always worked to find a way to fix things herself; and this is not unique only to Kate—Jack, Locke, Sawyer, and others fashion their lives around schemes devised to mend their broken lives. On the island she stops running just long enough to see the ways she is reliving her story and repeating the same mistakes. She is drawn to Sawyer, but for once, rather than living by her impulses, she attempts to examine the root causes of this desire and confesses them to an unconscious Sawyer, who she thinks may be on his deathbed. She asks tenderly, "Can you hear me? Sawyer?" And with that, her tone suddenly shifts from sweetness to perplexity; although she is physically addressing Sawyer, her words are meant for Wayne, her true father, whom, you may recall, she murdered in a fierce explosion:

> Wayne? I'm probably crazy and this doesn't matter, but maybe you're in there somehow. But you asked me a question. You asked me why . . . why I did it. It wasn't because you drove my father away, or the way you looked at me, or because you beat her. It's because I hated that you were a part of me . . . that I would never be good, that I would never have anything good. And every time that I look at Sawyer . . . every time I feel something for him . . . I see you, Wayne. And it makes me sick.

Kate finds herself irresistibly and fatally attracted to the one man on the island who reminds her of her abusive, belligerent, and broken father, which in turn reminds her that this same abusive, belligerent, and broken man is a part of her. All of us have an earthly father whose image we carry buried deep inside, an image that manifests itself in ways unrecognizable to us but nevertheless professes the touch of another human being. Sometimes this is a source of comfort; and others, as in the case of Kate, it's a burden to be shouldered. In this moment of vulnerability, we see Kate's worst fear: she may never be able to shake the influence of her father, and so she decides merely to outrun it, staying only a few steps ahead of his shadow. She is haunted by guilt—not the guilt of her actions, but the guilt of who she is, or who she may be. Like Sayid, Kate is frightened by her potential within, afraid that she is not (and will never be) good. And while we may root for Sawyer to end up with Kate, he serves as the constant reminder of her tendencies toward wildness; he is a relic of the traits she regrets inheriting. Sawyer, she believes (and he too), cannot change. The past is the present and the future, and so they must run together. "You run; I con," Sawyer tells her. "Tigers don't change their stripes." But here, again, we ask ourselves, how long is the arm of change? It's hard to argue that Kate and Sawyer remain static throughout the series: we watch them struggle and grow, both together and separately, into people we can admire . . . sometimes (which is better than never).

One of Kate's flashbacks occurs in "*Tabula Rasa*," which translates to "blank slate" and alludes to a theory proposed by seventeenth-century philosopher John Locke. While in philosophy it refers to empiricism, or the attainment of knowledge, on the island it's safe to say that it refers to simply a second chance. The slates of the Losties have been wiped clean. The island has given everyone, including Kate, a second chance and thus serves as a vehicle of redemption. When she tries to tell Jack what she did, he tells her that everyone deserves a fresh start. On the island, Kate changes from someone bold in her actions but fearful of commitment to someone morally sure of what's right and wrong, someone who can be a mother, someone who can take care of others. She assists Claire in the delivery of Aaron and encourages her, asserting, "This baby is all of ours." She recognizes the profound significance of a birth on the island, an unforgiving and unfamiliar terrain, and offers her own responsibility for the baby. Aaron may not be her child, but he represents everyone's new life together on the island—and specifically the beginning of Kate's change, which gives her freedom from her old ways. (Coincidentally, Aaron in the Bible served as a spokesman for his brother, Moses, and acted as a vehicle for the freedom of the Israelites from the Pharaoh.) Of course, we know that there is not one immediate moment of monumental change; instead—and this is the case for Kate—it is a process, a journey. Kate is far from perfect, but we see her develop an ethic, a moral sense she acts out consistently. In season five's controversial "Whatever Happened, Happened," young Ben is shot by Sayid. Kate knows that if left alone, Ben will die, and she cannot allow the death of a child to occur with no effort to stop it. So despite the fact that she knows who Ben Linus will become, she saves his life, keeping the path to the future we've already witnessed directly familiar. It's debatably moral, and while we can argue with the ethics, we must agree that the actions were thoughtful and Kate compassionate, rather than just passionate. She is evolving, growing, at once maturing and reverting to previous failures. No one knows if her growth will lead her to become a hero in season six, or maybe a faithful mother. One thing we do know is that men and women alike will be watching closely to see exactly who our Kate is to become.

James "Sawyer" Ford:
Patron Saint of Kindhearted Con Men

Whomever I have cheated I will pay back four times what I took.

—Zaccheus, in Luke 19:8

In season one we instinctively despise this long-haired Southern swindler who hoards food, medicine, weapons, or basically any useful thing he can get his hands on (except for sexy tank tops; the women seem to find an abundance of these). Sawyer begins to carve out his own hostile space on the island. Every other castaway seems to intuitively understand that their survival relies completely on their ability to care for one another and work together, but not Sawyer. He intends to become an island unto himself. His plan is simple: create a stockpile and a makeshift shelter, then read every book he can get his hands on. He assumes that with food, medicine, and shelter, his primary needs will be met, and the great stories can occupy his social desires. In fact, Sawyer might well have spent his entire island life immersed in a cheap novel if his eyes had allowed it. But reading without glasses is causing migraine headaches, and for the first time in his life, Sawyer is not capable of solving a problem on his own. In fact, the only person with the knowledge and ability to help is his nemesis, Jack. So what does Jack do? He determines that Sawyer is suffering from farsightedness, and Sayid then fashions a pair of reading glasses for Sawyer from salvaged spectacles. Headaches cured. But those glasses cure more than Sawyer's headaches; they lead him down a new path of understanding that he is not self-sufficient and that life in community is a better life than one of isolation.

Sawyer is the predictable bad guy, the rude-beyond-words jerk who, we believe, steals the inhaler right out of the mouth of a gasping blonde. He's the typical wrench in every plan to make island life better for everyone, and if he were ugly, the audience could assume he's slated for a quick, satisfying death within the first season. But ugly he is not. He's got those dimples, that six-pack, that distinctive smile and Southern charm; so instead he becomes every woman's dream. (Okay, maybe only those women who dream of saving the tortured bad boy, of being the *one* woman magical enough to change the frog into the prince.)

But bad boys don't ever change, do they? And do we even want them to? At least we gain understanding for Sawyer as the story of his sad childhood unfolds. Kate begins to discover his tragic secret by reading a tattered letter she finds in his pocket: "Dear Mr. Sawyer, you don't know who I am, but I know who you are and I know what you done. You had sex with my mother and then you stole my dad's money all away. So he got angry and he killed my mother and then he killed himself too. All I know is your name. But one of these days I'm going to find you, and

I'm going to give you this letter so you'll remember what you done to me. You killed my parents, Mr. Sawyer." We are all struggling with Kate to put this letter into a context and puzzle together the pieces of Sawyer's broken story. Did a young boy write this letter to him? Why does he carry it with him continually affixed to his back pocket? Suddenly it dawns on Kate (and the rest of us): "This letter wasn't written to you. You wrote this letter. Your name's not Sawyer, is it?"

In a wicked web of dysfunction Freud himself could not untangle, Sawyer has spent his life hating the man who seduced his mother, stole their life, and caused his father's murder-suicide. His anger completely consumes him, but his fixation does not result in the justice he dreamed of; instead, he becomes the man he despises, assuming this man's name and his singular gift of seducing women and swindling them for all they possess. Moreover, he believes there is no hope for change; redemption is impossible for his kind. He even projects the same hopelessness upon Kate: "You run; I con. Tigers don't change their stripes." But there are no tigers on this island, just fish and polar bears.

And Sawyer *does* change his stripes. One of the most satisfying pleasures of *Lost* is that we find characters who actually change and grow. Aside from classic literature and coming-of-age shows (which usually focus on only one main character), *Lost* is one of the very few TV narratives with people who grow in a positive direction, simultaneously regress in other directions, and yet stretch toward a healthier whole, on a truly lifelike, multidimensional scale.

Sawyer is the prime example. At the beginning he's a spiteful, rude-nickname generator with a criminal history, a revolting violent streak, and a severe allergy to wearing a shirt. But by the end of season five, he's stunningly grown into a true leader who keeps his jumpsuit on and even has a healthy, long-term relationship with Juliet. He admits this change to Kate when he says he was "no more ready to be her boyfriend than he was to be Clementine's daddy." But he is ready now, to be a good man to Juliet and a solid leader in the Dharma Initiative. He's an interesting foil to Jack's character, with his sudden inability (or unwillingness) to lead. Of course, Jack is changing too.

One question raised in *Lost*'s narrative of personal growth is, Are we ready for the ride? Watching characters like Sawyer change so deeply *does* something to us. We start asking ourselves: Do we want him to grow? Or do we relish the predictable bad guy? What do we do with people who were murderers, who were selfish, spiteful, and mean? Despite our previous leanings, it feels good to see Sawyer become a respectable, real man; we yearn for his full redemption.

Lost forces us to forgive, forget, and move forward,

believing in change and in hope. It's a lot like the gospel, really. It was the Sawyer types Jesus befriended in ancient days, and he wasn't afraid of nudity or vulgar speech either. In scandal after scandal, Jesus chose bad guys and sickos as friends and supporters, and true to form, they failed him, time and again. Jesus knew what troubled beginnings were all about. The miracle is that his love is extended to us in our angry, hateful, and shirtless state—not offered as a carrot on a stick for the person we each might become. Looking at Sawyer's sly grin, I think he's gotten a glimpse of this truth. And maybe after watching *Lost*, we can all face change and find real hope for the person in the mirror.

Man of Science, Man of Faith: Saint Jack and Saint John

Justice and power must be brought together, so that whatever is just may be powerful, and whatever is powerful may be just.

—Blaise Pascal, French mathematician, physicist, and philosopher (1623–1662)

Each and every character on *Lost* is intriguing, complex, and alluring. They draw us into their matchless stories in a way that is entirely their own. But none of the castaways stands alone. They have strengths that accentuate the individuality of their opposites. An English rock star picks mangoes with an African priest while a Korean mafioso builds a raft with a young black kid from urban America. The show manages to merge divergent cultures and differing personalities without looking staged like a Benetton advertisement. The characters accentuate one another; they play off of one another not only in dialogue but also by mere contrast. One of the most profound examples of foil characters (a character used to highlight a trait of another character by acting as its complete opposite) is the conflict between Jack Shephard, our resident "man of science," and John Locke, the "man of faith." While both of these characters have other foils (Jack, the responsible good citizen, versus Sawyer, the ne'er-do-well; and Locke versus Eko, two men whose faith is exercised differently), this is the most prominently represented and developed contrast in the series. Jack and John are, essentially, two sides of the same coin, but the coin in question here is not really leadership (where their tension often resides) but *doubt*. They are composed of the same stuff, but they deal with their belief and doubt so differently that it becomes hard to not look at them as dueling entities.

Locke, unlike Jack, wants desperately to believe in the island, in Jacob, in a higher being, a personal God to give meaning to the large and small tragedies of life. Most of the time, he can take a leap of faith. But then again, is this faith concrete or a fleeting sensation? Sometimes John finds himself extending a pleading hand and receiving nothing in return but chaff and dust. Of course, the island's ways are not John's ways, and so John occasionally but inevitably just misses what the island is trying to tell him. What he believes to be there is still there—it's just eclipsed by John himself. When this happens, however, we see the breakdown of the impenetrable Locke. He's the man of faith to Jack's man of science, yes, but even the representative of faith can falter. Ben explains that to Jack in season five, as they ponder a great painting of Doubting Thomas, that Thomas was faithful to Jesus, but when Christ rose from the grave, the apostle just couldn't wrap his mind around it—and suddenly doubt was born. Thomas needed proof; he needed to be able to touch his Lord and feel that it was real. Again, we see the physical manifestation of an organic, struggling faith, and often the doubt blooms into something stronger and more beautiful.

It's the same for John Locke. His faith does not fade; instead it disappears completely (if only momentarily and most often privately) but regenerates holistically. After the death of Boone in season one, Locke pounds on the locked hatch and demands answers to why this happened. He cries and strikes out, but eventually has a revelation that the death of Boone was a sacrifice the island demanded, a declaration severe and cold; but in the wake of this we see the rebirth of John's faith. It happens again at the end of season two: Mr. Eko has taken John's place as token island mystic, leaving John an injured (remember, he hurts his leg in the hatch) man of broken faith. Mr. Eko believes the map that John saw in the black light during the hatch's lockdown is a sign sent from Yemi, his dead brother. He asks for it and John gives it angrily, telling him that it is nothing more than a fleeting memory, a piece of trash with no intrinsic or even extrinsic value. John now believes that pushing the button in the hatch is a joke, that it is meaningless. "I was never meant to do anything," he says, echoing the words of King Solomon in Ecclesiastes, who said, "Everything is meaningless (NIV)." Mr. Eko tries to convince him otherwise but cannot; John refuses to push the button, and the hatch implodes. For each crisis of faith, the ramifications become more severe.

C. S. Lewis wrote that pain is God's megaphone to rouse a deaf world; for John Locke, it takes an explosion.

In season five we find John Locke hoping and believing beyond reason (and isn't that what faith ultimately is about?) that Christian Shephard's commission—that it's up to Locke to save the island by bringing the Oceanic 6 back to it—is true: he does not yet *believe* it, but he is attempting to work it out in a physical way by teleporting off the island and searching all over the world for the Oceanic 6. He has nothing concrete to base this on, only a familiar apparition appearing to him in a moment forced to its crisis; after all, the Christian of the island may be his own hallucination . . . the result of an undigested bit of mango or a bad Dharma Initiative hot dog. But, John, unlike Jack, as we see time and time again, merely chooses to act on a tenuous belief. He ultimately seems to fail in reuniting the band, so to speak, and now his faith seems stretched gossamer thin over a crevasse of doubt so deep it seems bottomless. This, as we have seen, leads to Locke's attempted suicide. The image of Locke standing on the shabby coffee table with a noose around his neck becomes a visual reminder of what doubt, left to fester on its own with no challenges, can do. It can undo us; it can unravel us; it can shake us and unnerve us until we find ourselves on the precipice of unbelief.

Locke is the man of faith whose faith is not as steadfast

as he would like it to be, and if the faith on which he places his entire existence is rocked, then what he banks on—his specialness—is the antithesis of what he worked himself up to believe: it is, essentially, a misinterpretation of his entire life. Where we are now with *Lost*, with John Locke and his faith, is yet to be seen. John has doubts; he questions the authenticity of his destiny; he struggles. We wait now and see how, or if, John has crossed over into the tremulous realm of faith once again. *Time*'s TV critic James Poniewozik writes:

> John Locke is *Lost*'s man of faith. But he's not, really, not entirely. He certainly has faith, in the Island, in the unexplained, but he also has doubt; his faith is constantly shaken and never as absolute as he wants it to be. When he goes to persuade Jack that he needs to go back to the Island, you can see in his searching popeyes that some part of him also wants to persuade himself—that he is special, that his "destiny" is not a mistake, that he's not being swindled again. (Think about it: if one character on *Lost* has reason to have no faith, in anything or anyone, it's John Locke.)[1]

Remember the scene where he gets ready to hang himself? He's not going into this calmly, as some sort of stoic sacrifice; he's been told by Richard Alpert that he must die to save the island, but he doesn't entirely believe it, doesn't entirely want to. You can see the despair in his eyes, the fear. He wants to die; he doesn't want to die. The man of faith is a man of doubt.

Jack's doubt is very different. The nineteenth-century philosopher William Kingdon Clifford asserted, "It is wrong, always, everywhere, and for anyone, to believe anything upon insufficient evidence."[2] This maxim holds true for Jack, and so he finds himself standing at the same precipice of unbelief. He is not the doubter who struggles; he does not fight. He accepts. But at the end of it all, will Jack become a believer? We see a few shining moments of trust after he leaves the island with absolute certainty and refuses to waver about the possibility that they were destined to remain. So how is it that Jack has picked up on the mission of John Locke to return the Oceanic 6 to the island—and made that mission his own? In the end, he remains a skeptic . . . or is it possible he has become a seeker, abandoning his cynicism and actively pursuing the kind of truth that leads to faith? As he deeply ponders Caravaggio's painting *The Incredulity of St. Thomas*, Jack asks Ben if Thomas believed when he touched Jesus' wounds. To which Ben replies, "Of course he did. Sooner or later everyone believes." Will Jack embrace faith? Will his Thomaslike doubts spur him on in a discovery of a lasting faith? If he believes, will it be reason or experience that guides him to a new spiritual home? Either way, I suppose that Jack has it in him to believe; he can hear the knocking, and now he must decide how to answer the call.

Locke and the Island:
John Locke (1632–1704)

Have you ever been hurt and the place tries to heal a bit,
and you just pull the scar off of it over and over again?

—Rosa Parks, American civil-rights activist (1913–2005)

All of *Lost*'s viewers know that names are important in this television series. Through the use of historical, philosophical, and religious allusions, the writers of the show offer a little insight into who it is the characters really are—basically, it's like a puzzle that allows us to show off in front of our friends just how smart we are. The writers draw much from the history of the Jewish people, often pulling the story line into a parallel track with the biblical narrative and at other times offering a tip of the hat to the most storied characters of the Bible, or a great scientist, or an important philosopher. The writers that bring us *Lost* are often like Hebrew parents: they name their children carefully, after much thought and prayer. Because the Hebrews believed that a name possessed an unusual power to both guide one's destiny and offer a description of the path one would journey, naming a child was not to be taken lightly. To understand any character on this magical island, you must consider his or her name; many correspond with names or concepts that come directly from the Bible and often from history, such as Benjamin (the son of Jacob in Genesis) and Shephard (a metaphor for leadership and a direct link to Jesus).

John Locke has the most obvious reference because his name is actually the same as that of perhaps the greatest English philosopher of the modern period.

The philosopher John Locke (for the sake of clarity, whenever I mention the character Locke in *this* chapter, I'll refer to him as Lost Locke) held the search for truth as the highest good for which a human could strive, and this value was intrinsically related to his Christian faith; however, he viewed his religion rationally, condemning those who believed in God but had no foundation of faith. In other words, for Locke, God was real but belief was only valid if you could explain why. He held that rationalism and theism were not mutually exclusive and could exist together and support one another. God, he wrote, uses reason as a way to reveal himself to us.

Locke's main contributions are composed of three philosophical tenets: first, the idea of *tabula rasa*; second, the social-contract theory; and finally, empiricism. All of these philosophical tenets are explored on *Lost* through the lives of different characters in ways that make the concepts much more interesting than any of John Locke's philosophical essays!

Does *tabula rasa* sound familiar? It's been touched upon before in another chapter (and is the name of a Kate-centric episode), so we won't spend time on it here, but to refresh your memory in philosophy, it refers to the idea of the mind being a blank slate when we are born. That is, we don't have any ideas or knowledge about anything when we come into the world; therefore everything that we do learn comes from experience outside of the womb. But, before any of you pregnant mothers out there get upset, many books have been published since Locke's death that describe the ways children are shaped *in utero*. An example of the tabula rasa in *Lost* is when we also see Karl, Alex's boyfriend, strapped into a chair as he is bombarded with aural and visual stimuli in a sort of brainwashing effort to wash his slate clean.

Social-contract theory enacted is when people give up some rights to a higher authority or power in order to maintain social order; in return, a citizen has certain natural rights that he or she is not asked to relinquish. If it sounds confusing—and it probably does, because all philosophy sounds confusing at first—there will be a *Lost*-related example shortly following that will clarify any consternation.

These last two premises lead into empiricism, or the idea that knowledge arises from experience. It empha- sizes sensory perception as key to developing knowledge. John Locke gave this example to demonstrate empiri- cism: A child in a black and white room won't know anything else but black and white, but can become aware of other things, although he might not actually *know* of them. His other experiences in learning and gaining knowledge dictate that if there are two colors, there could possibly be more than two. Even in this room with only black and white, he can imagine what other shades and hues might look like. The reason we are aware of universal truths is that we share a similar experience, leading to similar knowledge. We "know" about things because we experience similar things.

Lost Locke is the philosophical opposite of Jack Shephard. Both embody leadership characteristics and often find themselves in contention with one another. While Jack sees himself as a "shepherd" with the responsibility to lead his people based on his own moral authority, Lost Locke represents the social-contract theory: he answers to a higher power (the island) and has given up some rights (i.e., he has traded in self-reliance for loyalty to the island) in order to maintain what he perceives to be the proper societal order. Lost Locke's epistemology has progressed from empiricism to blind faith; through his experiences in life, he has come to have faith in the old adage, "Everything happens for a reason." Now he no longer needs proof (except for the times his faith in the island falters) and can rely on his past sensory perceptions to tell him what is true.

For example, take this situation: Lost Locke drugs Boone, who then has a cryptic hallucination that may or may not have some sort of bigger meaning. He tells Boone this is an experience Boone needed for his development on the island. Boone agrees. This scenario is an example of empirical knowledge: Boone's belief stems from a sensory perception. He experiences something and gains an idea of it, which then leads to a predisposition of knowledge. An idea is birthed through two senses: first, an external sense (the initial sensation), and then an internal sense (reflection on the sensation).

Still confusing? Here's another example. In "Lockdown," a season two episode, Lost Locke sees a mysterious map on the wall of the hatch and has only a few minutes to remember what he sees on that wall before the image is gone again. As he tries to transcribe what he remembers of the map, he becomes more and more frustrated. Despite Eko's attempt to help figure out the map in relation to the island, Locke has a crisis of confidence. "Here," he says angrily, shoving the map into Eko's hand, "take this. It's a memory. Ten seconds and nothing else." Experiences become memories, and memories become ideas, or imprints of primary sensations. John experiences seeing a map on the wall; he remembers it enough to re-create the image, and he then begins thinking about *what* this map might mean; he has an idea that the map is relevant to the island and corresponds to what he has already experienced. Eventually we process the idea and turn the idea into knowledge, or belief. But ultimately we only know our ideas, and the rest of what we know (or think we know) comes from faith.

Jack's priority is to protect his people; Lost Locke's priority is to protect the island. He reveres the island and emphasizes the knowledge he is continually granted by the island; he plays the faithful mystic to Jack's doubting pragmatist. He has a deeper understanding of the earth beneath his feet. It is the spiritual world that interests Lost Locke. He denies the physical realm for the intangible world of faith and sees knowledge as a special privilege, something that separates some people from others. It must be earned, and Lost Locke, much like his historical namesake, is willing to sacrifice his physical being in order to adhere to the island's demands.

In 1704 the philosopher John Locke left this earth. But he understood that his ideas and writings would continue to shape culture long after he passed. His epitaph reads:

Stop Traveller

Near this place lies JOHN LOCKE. If you are wondering what kind of man he was, he answers that he was contented with his modest lot. Bred a scholar, he made his learning subservient only to the cause of truth. You will learn this from his writings, which will show you everything about him more truthfully than the suspect praises of an epitaph. His virtues, if indeed he had any, were too slight to be lauded by him or to be an example to you. Let his vices be buried with him. Of virtue you have an example in the gospels, should you desire it; of vice would there were none for you; of mortality surely you have one here and everywhere, and may you learn from it. That he was born on the 29th of August in the year of our Lord 1632 and that he died on the 28th of October in the year of our Lord 1704 this tablet, which itself will soon perish, is a record.[1]

His writings have influenced the U.S. Constitution, Martin Luther King Jr., Gandhi, Abraham Lincoln, and likely every prominent thinker of the last three hundred years. If you want to read his work, I suggest you begin with "A Letter Concerning Toleration," which was written in 1689. Despite its age you will find a riveting assessment of the difference between those who come to faith through an authority that is earned through sacrificial love, and those who convert under the influence of power structures that wield violence. In this letter you will hear a voice and a message that sounds as contemporary as Bono. Locke could have never imagined that his ideas would be explored apart from his textual work by millions of people watching a television narrative that would be routinely downloaded on iTunes. The genre has changed, but the wisdom sought by both of our John Lockes is still desperately needed today. So thank you to the writers and creators of *Lost* for giving us an alternative to an hour of Geraldo Rivera that will actually lead us to think and pick up an essay written by a wig-wearing man from the 1600s. Who would have guessed all this could come from a story of a cadre of beautiful people stranded on an island?

Jack Shephard: Patron Saint of Wounded Healers

I'm often called an old-fashioned modernist. But the modernists had the absurd idea that architecture could heal the world. That's impossible. And today nobody expects architects to have these grand visions anymore.

—Thom Mayne, American architect

Jack is not only a physician—he is the rock star of physicians. Surgeons study longer and spend a virtual lifetime in a grueling residency. Anytime you lay down on a cold O.R. table in the United States and begin to count backwards as a mask covers your face, you can rest assured that the surgeon who will incise your soft tissue is well educated and has risen to the top tier of his or her privileged profession. That said, most surgeons humbly lay down their scalpels in the presence of a great spinal surgeon—because when one navigates the complexities of the spinal column, there is no room for mistakes. The hand must perfectly execute every intention of the brain; otherwise the patient is doomed to paralysis, respiratory failure, or death. A spinal surgeon cannot afford to have an off day.

Jack Shephard is a spinal surgeon, among the world's best. This kind of pressure does not foster a sense of humility or an acceptance of self-deprecation. Jack's patients do not want him to be fallible; they expect a skill that is godlike. So we need not be scandalized by his so-called God complex—the belief that he is capable of fixing even the direst tribulations faced by these castaways. Jack is who we want him to be, and when he fails he does not confess his weakness; he picks up the bottle or a prescription drug and refuses to accept failure.

We have a general inclination to think about Jack in relation only to other characters: he's Kate's love interest; he's the opposite of Sawyer; he's also the anti-Locke. Our other tendency is to label him nicely and neatly as the chosen leader of the castaways. These are all valid, all provide a plethora of arguments in their favor—but they all fall a bit short. Eventually Jack develops past these limitations into someone who serves as a testament to himself, rather than as a foil for Locke and Sawyer. Jack is best understood when we simply observe him on his own, when we examine his habits, listen to the things he says.

Yes, Jack is the leader. From the very beginning the survivors gravitate toward him, expecting that if they were to be saved, he would be the one capable of doing so. In the first few minutes of the pilot episode, it seems that Jack has already saved the lives of no less than six people. And he wants to save them; he embraces the role bestowed upon him by his peers, his people. But we don't always make the right choices. (It's not just Americans who mess up; it's the human race.) Given this distinctly human quality, then, it becomes a likely possibility that perhaps the survivors of 815 make a mistake and give the keys to the city to the wrong candidate.

Jack plays the part of the leader well: he is confident, he is decisive, he's got very cool tattoos that are part of an even better story of a gang beating he endured in Thailand . . . and in the real world Jack was a star spinal surgeon, next in line to inherit his own father's medical acclaim. He was born to save lives. He was born to fix things. Take his relationship with his estranged ex-wife, Sarah, for example. Sarah was Jack's patient, the victim of an accident that left her paralyzed from the waist down. Jack becomes emotionally invested in her case and promises her the impossible—that he will heal her—and eventually, miraculously, Sarah does regain the ability to walk. Later she falls in love, marries Jack—and falls out of love. On her way out the door and out of his life, Sarah looks back at Jack and says, "Look at it this way: now you have something to fix." This is both Jack's gift and curse. He is blessed with this intense need to heal, to fix, to correct a wrong; yet this single-minded focus warps his view of life, himself, and his purpose.

In Jack's worldview, everything is achievable through tangible, human ability: he *is* a man of faith; it's just that his faith is fairly humanistic. He has no need for things he cannot see because he has his hands. He has his feet. He has his brain, and this is all he needs. Jack denies the possibility of what may lie behind the curtain. In the season four finale, as Jack is preparing to leave the island,

Locke asks Jack to stay behind with him, an idea at which Jack readily scoffs. They begin a discussion, the gist of which, although it manifests itself as a clashing of titans, really reveals more profound thought:

> **JACK:** What am I *supposed* to do? . . . What was it you said on our way back to the hatch? That crashing here was our destiny? . . . It's an island. It doesn't need protection.
>
> **LOCKE:** An island? No, it's a place where miracles happen.
>
> **JACK:** There are no such things as miracles.
>
> **LOCKE:** Well, we'll have to wait and see which one of us is right . . . You'll have to lie to the people [when you get back, about what has happened]. Lie to them, Jack. If you do it half as well as you lie to yourself, they'll believe you.

Jack cannot allow himself to believe in miracles simply because they are humanly inexplicable. There is no rationale. There is nothing Jack could do to produce a miracle; therefore they must not exist. If there is a higher force that heals, rescues, and resurrects, then what role is he to play? Although (according to Locke) Jack has the ability to believe, he hears the knocking at the door but he does not permit himself to answer it—yet. He rejects the help of anyone else because, after all, he is the leader. In season four Jack is struck with appendicitis, but he refuses to stop leading. Juliet finally convinces him to allow her to operate on him, but he demands to be awake so that he can talk her through it. He can't let go; he must maintain at the very least the illusion of control. Similarly, in the first flash-forward we see on the show, we watch as Jack quietly self-destructs; another doctor tries to intervene, attempting to reassure Jack that he is only hoping to help. Jack lashes back and says, "You can't help me!"

It's no wonder he would feel this way. Think about every situation in which you have an authority figure, someone you regard as your leader. We tend to think of our leaders as people beyond the need of help; we ritually take away the things that make them human. Remember as a child the first time you saw one of your teachers in an outside setting? It was a little shocking—sort of like seeing a dog walk on its hind legs, right? That's because we place people who are leaders into categories beyond the capacity of natural human facilities. Jack is a victim of this sort of thinking, and he has allowed it to shape who he has become. He is a person who, although he is capable of belief in the less-tangible things, cannot allow himself to exercise this belief because it may be seen as a sign of weakness, a breach of self-confidence. The tattoo on his shoulder is a label that speaks over Jack for life: "He walks among us, but is not one of us."

Jack is the presumed leader on the island, but because of the hindrances Jack has regarding his role, he isn't the chosen one. He shows the capabilities of being a fine leader, but when it comes down to it, we all need a leader with hope. Jack *seems* to have hope . . . but it gets lost in his focus on pragmatism and is strangled by his logic. This is not to say that Jack is a lost cause; he has potential, and even now, as we enter into the final season, Jack has changed. We watch him melt down in front of Kate, confessing that they made a mistake, that they had a purpose there on the island, that they have one now, that there is a greater plan in motion of which they are a part. He's a person who can subscribe to the idea of destiny, to the notion of belief. There is no question that Jack yearns to be an instrument of redemption, and coupled with his newfound capacity to believe, he can fully become an agent of truth because he's experienced authentic change.

Just like Jack, we are all called to be movers and shakers in the story of faith—but that doesn't always mean we are all the big-shot leaders, or the ones who do the "important" things. In 1 Corinthians 12, Paul wrote that we are all a part of the church, a part of the body of Christ, but we are also all diverse within this unity, and in this diversity, we find necessity:

Just as a body is one whole made up of many different parts, and all the different parts comprise the one body, so it is with our Liberating King. We were all ceremonially washed together into one body by one Spirit. No matter our heritage—Jew or Greek, insider or outsider— no matter our status—oppressed or free—we were all given the one Spirit to drink. Here's why: the body is not made of one large part but of many different parts. Would it seem right for the foot to cry, "I am not a hand, so I couldn't be part of this body"? Even if it did, it wouldn't be any less joined to the body. And what about an ear? If an ear started to whine, "I am not an eye; I shouldn't be attached to this body," in all its pouting, it is still part of the body. Imagine the entire body as an eye. How would a giant eye have the sense to hear? And if the entire body were an ear, how would it have the sense to smell? This is where God comes in. God has meticulously put this body together; He placed each part in the exact place to perform the exact function He wanted. If all members were a single part, where would the body be? So now, many members function within the one body. The eye cannot wail at the hand, "I have no need for you," nor could the head bellow at the feet, "I won't go one more step with you." It's actually the opposite. The members who seem to have the weaker functions are necessary to keep the body moving; the body parts that seem less important we treat as some of the most valuable, and those unfit, untamed, unpresentable members we treat with an even greater modesty. That's something the more presentable members don't need. But God designed the body in such a way that greater significance is given to the seemingly insignificant part. That way there should be no division in the body; instead, all the parts mutually depend on and care for one another. If one part is suffering, then all the members suffer alongside it. If one member is honored, then all the members celebrate alongside it. You are the body of our Liberating King; each and every one of you is a vital member. (vv. 12–27)

Not everyone gets to be or—better said—*has to be* the chosen leader, and sometimes, like Jack, we may struggle for it and try to force that role into becoming our destiny. But when we realize that the various paths laid out for us are all special, that we are all given unique gifts, we can truly accept who we are called to be. Jack does this in season five; he begins the journey toward a more transcendent purpose, toward belief, and toward redemption. He allows himself to truly become an instrument for change. He has expanded his vision to a bigger picture and has agreed to work in alignment with something greater. It is the same for us as people who have accepted the heart and mission of God through his Son, Jesus: we are now the hands and feet of his movement and thus continue his work of turning the world upside down.

In the fifth season we meet a new Jack, one who is no longer scheming and planning how to outwit the island. This new Jack speaks of the unspeakable: destiny. He wants no part in leading and seems truly contented to follow. The man who felt he had to control everything is now trusting more as circumstances arise, letting his intuition and his peers guide him on the path of salvation. This newfound humility was hard earned and comes only with the sting of failure.

Jack leaves the island of his own will. Although he is warned that leaving is a mistake, he leaves with a sense of a mission completed, having saved a handful of Losties— but like each one of us, Jack makes his own path. Like the lost son in Luke 15, he takes his Oceanic inheritance and chooses to pilot his own life. With money in his pocket, a diploma on his wall, and the love of a beautiful woman, he believes he is assured the pleasures and successes of the world.

But those pleasures and successes fail to satisfy. In the three years that pass before he is shown a way to return to the island, Jack spirals down from his penthouse lifestyle to live and look like any homeless man on the streets of the California city where he lives. Desperation ultimately leads him to come home (home to this island he now concludes he never should have left) and assume a new position . . . as a Dharma "work man," which amounts to little more than a janitor. His island homecoming celebration is still to come, but if my intuition serves me well, I believe season six will bring Jack the welcome-home party of a lifetime, and a new sense of who he is and what it is he is truly *called* to be. He returns home, like the lost son, abandoning his arrogance and selfishness to embrace a new humility—and, for the first time in his life, a chance to give and receive love.

Jesus Wrote a Best Seller

A woman in Mexico wanted me to heal her. But I can't heal anybody. I just put my hand on her and said, "Thank you for seeing the film."

—Jim Caviezel, American actor

When confronted by a group of people enslaved by the legalism of religion but lacking in the more transcendent gifts of faith, hope, and love, Jesus did not punish them for their ignorance and self-importance; instead he told them a story. If ABC's version of *Lost* garnered twenty-three million viewers, and Coldplay's versions of "Lost?" and "Lost!" sold sixteen million downloads on iTunes alone, then it is hard to imagine another story about lost-ness capturing a greater market share or reaching a higher acclaim. But Jesus seems to be the first storyteller to captivate large audiences (say, seventy-five billion?) with a series of stories all about this abject quality of being missing or adrift or just plain lost. In Luke chapter 15, Jesus masterfully wove together three stories: one told of a lost sheep, another a lost coin, and finally, most profoundly, one spoke of a lost son. In the midst of signs, miracles, and stories about the kingdom, Jesus seemed to break from the script when he began this succession of stories. What could have prompted such a radical departure?

Based on the historical context and the Pharisees Jesus addresses in this story, some scholars believe Jesus may have been directly responding to a common maxim among this religious crowd that, loosely translated, says, "Heaven rejoices when one of these sinners is condemned to hell." Christianity (that is, the devotion to following the ways of Jesus) is about love, forgiveness, and reconciliation. Religion is about celebrating the knowledge that you are right, reveling in self-satisfaction, enjoying your superiority, and looking down on the unenlightened. It may seem a bit of an understatement to say that the world needs more Christianity and less religion, but it is such a valid and bold assertion that it can never be uttered often enough.

This us-versus-them mentality, this adherence to segregation, is another example of the kind of duality that runs through the stories that we know collectively as *Lost*. It was common to the Pharisees and remains prevalent for and relevant to all of us, even to the Losties who see themselves as completely different from the Others. Over the seasons this line has blurred a bit, but for the most part all of our original castaways tend to think of things on the island in terms of "our people" and "their people." The castaways are the good people, and the Others are just plain bad; of course, the Others understand the situation to be exactly the opposite. Take the premiere episode of season three, "A Tale of Two Cities." From the onset, we know that there will be, essentially, two cities, which we can assume will represent two sides of a given spectrum; of course, the two cities in question are those of the Others, who live in the suburbs of the island and hold book club meetings, and the Losties, who, as we all know, are still wandering in the wilderness. Previously in the series, Locke goes on a verbal tirade against the Others, listing each of the moral wrongs they have committed: they have lied, they have killed, they have stolen. These, he says, are *bad* people; however, all of these abominations have likewise been committed by all of our favorite castaways. Similarly, Jack, held in captivity by the Others, enumerates yet another list of malfeasances, and sums it up with this judgment in the episode "Stranger in a Strange Land": "*That's* the kind of people I think you are." Tom, the slightly overweight Other with white hair who first sported a fake beard to kidnap Walt, retorts, "See this glass house you're living in, Jack? Maybe I should get you some stones."

Perhaps, after all, the differences are not as great as we perceive—or as we hope—them to be. But instead of facing these, what do we do with people we consider to be Others? We lock them up, we study them—but to understand them, all we really need to do is examine ourselves, because the same heart, as broken and misguided as it may be, beats emphatically in all of us. But this equally and alternately scares us and convicts us, so instead of naming it, we point fingers at it and protest too much that *we are not the same*. Remember Amira, the woman Sayid allegedly tortured in Iraq? She tells an anecdote about saving a cat being tormented by a group of children, and finishes it by asserting that as humanity, "we are all capable of doing what those children did to that cat." Likewise, Sayid says early in season one that "there are worse things to fear than what's in the jungle."

Again, we split ourselves up into "us" and "others"— in spite of the fact that we all have the same heart. We are governed by similar motivations; we are enslaved to the human condition, the heart of darkness that binds us together in the jungle. And it is no mystery where this mentality can take us. It leads from separation to hatred to violence: we see it in Rwanda, Sudan, Hitler's Third Reich, and the small-scale fictional genocide of the Dharma Initiative at the hands of the Others. Genocides begin with these kinds of divisions. It does not always lead to murder, but, as Jesus reminds us, we have more to worry about than just murder: "Anyone who is angry with his brother will be judged for his anger. Anyone who taunts his friend, speaks contemptuously toward him, or calls him 'Loser' or 'Fool' or 'Scum,' will have to answer to the high court. And anyone who calls his brother a fool may find himself in the fires of hell" (Matthew 5:22). Jesus was no fan of the self-righteous.

How did Jesus address this mentality among the Pharisees who saw themselves as better than the "lost ones"? He told an epic story that negated all their pre-conceptions and explained why he was spending so much time with the ancient Others. In Luke 15 we're told:

Jesus became increasingly popular among notorious sinners—tax collectors and other social outcasts. The Pharisees and religious scholars noticed this.

Pharisees and Religious Scholars: This man welcomes immoral people and enjoys their company over a meal!

Jesus (with another parable): Wouldn't every single one of you, if you have 100 sheep and lose one, leave the 99 in their grazing lands and go out searching for the lost sheep until you find it? When you find the lost sheep, wouldn't you hoist it up on your shoulders, feeling wonderful? And when you go home, wouldn't you call together your friends and neighbors? Wouldn't you say, "Come over and celebrate with me, because I've found my lost sheep"? This is how it is in heaven. They're happier over one sinner who changes his way of life than they are over 99 good and just people who don't need to change their ways of life. (vv. 1–7)

If anything is clear in the gospel of Luke, it is that a new kingdom is emerging, and in that kingdom the lost ones are not despised; they are beloved. The stories of Jesus will shed more light on the insights found in the stories of *Lost*, but if redemption lies in our future, we must begin to see ourselves as we truly are and leave behind the arrogance and self-righteousness we so easily embody. If you are anything like me, you likely read through Luke 15 the first time with thoughts of all of the people who really needed to hear Jesus' discussion of this subject. As I started to list out the names of judgmental people I know, somewhere deep within I was commending myself for not being as pompous, pretentious, or unapproachable as the Pharisees and the haughty people on my "poor sinners" list. *Silence.* The Spirit cut through me like a knife, and my arrogance turned to tears. Jesus was speaking to me in these stories, and I believe he will speak to you if you take the time to listen.

In the coming chapters we will explore the deep connection between the "lost" stories of Jesus and *Lost*, and you may hear a strong and gentle reprimand in your ear, not unlike the scolding Brennan Manning offered to a brother. The solution, he says, is "simple, my dear fellow! Your trouble is you have your halo on too tight. All we need to do is to loosen it a bit. The trouble with our ideals is that if we live up to all of them, we become impossible to live with. The tilted halo of the saved sinner is worn loosely and with easy grace. We have discovered that the cross accomplished far more than revealing the love of God."[1] Amen.

Eko: Patron Saint of Warlord Priests

Do not abandon yourselves to despair. We are the
Easter people and hallelujah is our song.

—John Paul II, Polish-born pope of the Catholic Church (1920–2005)

If ever there was a lost sheep in need of rescue, it is vulnerable young Eko, drifting alone in a dangerous land. His flight from safety began as a young child. In Eko's first flashback, we watch as he is forced to make a drastic decision that will alter the course of two lives: his own and his younger brother Yemi's. Africa is plagued by violence, and for Eko and Yemi, their homeland Nigeria is no exception. In the fictional world of *Lost*, a local gang terrorizes Eko's small village, and one day the leader of the gang drags a man to his knees, puts a pistol in the child Yemi's hands, and tells Yemi that he must shoot this man or be killed himself. As Yemi stands frozen and unable to act, Eko steps up, takes the gun, and pulls the trigger, killing the man and sentencing himself to a nefarious future. But is Eko to blame for saving his younger brother from becoming a murderer? The man was undoubtedly going to die, and quite possibly Yemi as well. What's frustrating here is that what seems right is still wrong. No matter how hard we try, we cannot reconcile the logic of the mind to the resonating truth spoken by the Spirit in our hearts. Murder is wrong . . . but is it also true that Eko saved a life that day?

Riveting stories like Eko's remind us of great truths. Children are a sacred trust, a blessing from God to be nurtured with love, instructed with discipline, and led with great wisdom. Children are born with vast potential, but the broken realities of this world and the global community's failure to protect children make the future both uncertain and frightening. We have a tendency to refer to the world's children as our future (hum a Whitney Houston song quietly as you read this paragraph), our greatest natural resource, and so on, but global reality tells us this is less a heartfelt belief and more a trite cliché. The world is filled with stories of not only neglect but also the abuse and exploitation of those we regard as the leaders, the innovators, the mothers, the fathers—the caretakers—of tomorrow.

Exploitation of children, both sexually and economically, has become one of the most pressing atrocities our world must confront. It is the single most gruesome problem for which we have yet to find an adequate, absolute solution. The numbers of children who suffer each year from some sort of exploitation, whether involuntary servitude, sexual bondage, forced labor, or coerced participation as soldiers, are so vast that they often leave us numb rather than spur us to action. It is estimated that more than twenty-seven million people are currently living in slavery and that more than half those slaves are children. In Nigeria alone—a

BAC~CHUS

FE~ LIX

4
8
15

42
23
16

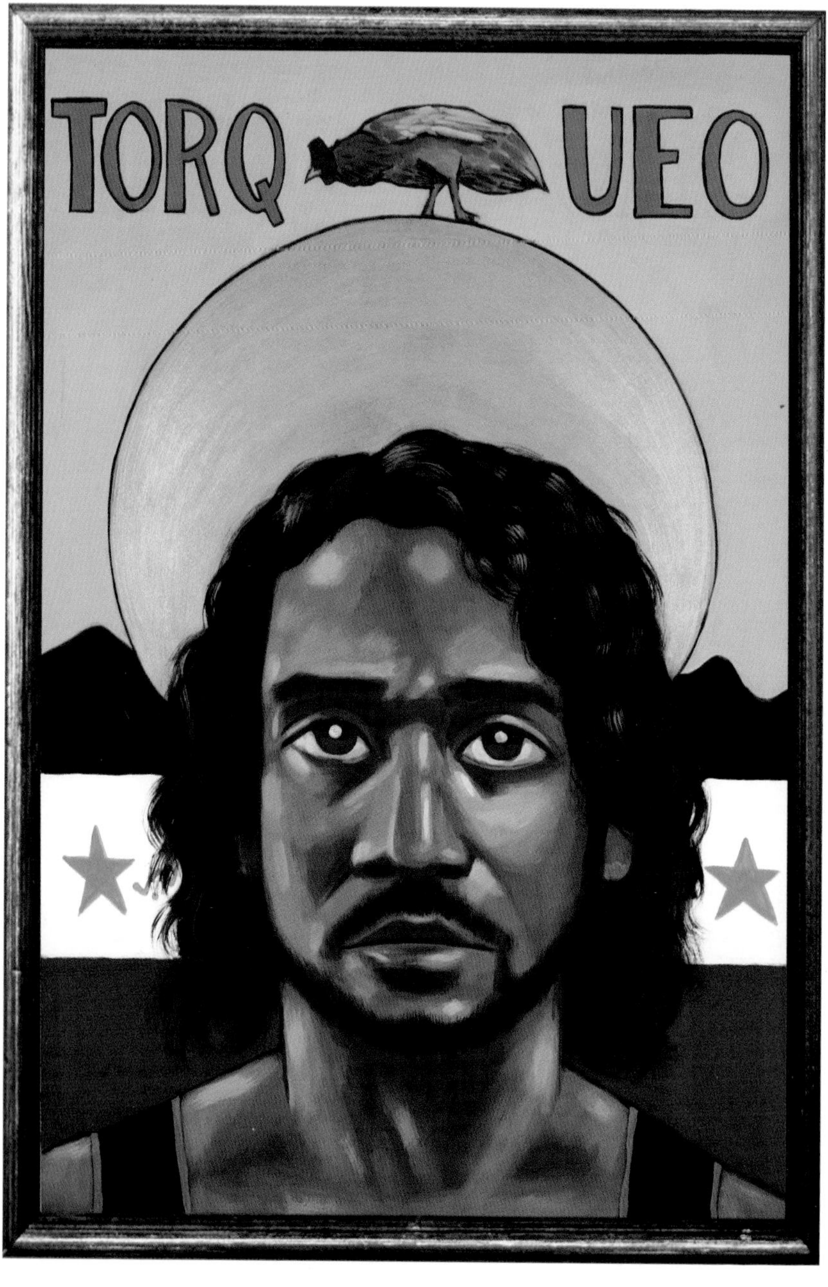
TORQ UEO

TYRANNUS

UM- 💍 BRA

country home not only to *Lost*'s enigmatic Eko but also to a hotbed of violent religious conflict—it has been reported by the National Agency for Prohibition and Trafficking in Persons and Other Related Matters that approximately fifteen million Nigerian children have been abducted and moved from a rural to an urban environment for child labor or slavery purposes. Furthermore, as *Lost* depicted, Nigeria unwillingly plays host to many gangs that often have a greater influence on the country than the government—and while most of these gangs and armed vigilante groups include members as young as eighteen, many groups, including the Egbesu Boys of the Niger Delta, have been known to recruit children under the age of sixteen. The world of today's child is rough, frightening, and precarious: the trauma inflicted on children, particularly these child combatants, has lifelong physical and psychological ramifications. While we can relax in the knowledge that Eko's disturbing childhood is fictional, we must be aware that stories like Eko's unfold daily without notice by more affluent, more "civilized" countries.

In so many ways, children have been left to fend for themselves, and through our own neglect or complacency, we have allowed them to become easy prey for the dark forces that civilized people would rather ignore than confront. Eko stands before us as nothing short of a warlord, a killer both menacing and scrupulous. This

is a man who, carefully weighing his options and meticulously predicting the order of events to follow, intimidates
his brother Yemi, a devoted priest, with violence against
innocent parishioners if he does not ordain Eko's crew
of drug traffickers as priests so they can smuggle heroin
encased in small ceramic statues of the Virgin Mary. The
symbol of the virgin who birthed salvation and forgiveness to mankind becomes a vessel of addiction, slavery,
and bondage; what transgression could be greater? Yet
Yemi sees this sacrilege as a lesser offense compared to
violence against women and children, so he concedes.
What kind of man could threaten his only brother, a
pious man of faith, and speak softly in his ear promises
of brutality? The answer, of course, is the kind of man
Eko is, so vicious that even fellow criminals whisper that
this brutal warlord is a man "who has no soul." And how
could it be that machinations with evil intentions could
be used for good in Eko's life?

Just watch. After Eko convinces Yemi to allow his men
to borrow priest's cassocks from the church, they board a
plane to fly the drugs across the border; at the last minute,
Yemi is killed in crossfire between the smugglers and
government forces. Eko is left behind and—through an
assumption of "the clothes make the man"—is mistaken for
a priest, a role he eventually embraces in his community.
And so a new chapter in Eko's life begins as he becomes,

however erroneously, a priest. The warlord kills no longer and instead blesses the holy sacraments each week, offering bread and wine to sinners seeking forgiveness. In a miraculous turn of events, the lost sheep is brought home.

On the island, however, priestly garb no longer sets Eko apart as a holy man, and his knowledge of Scripture is deficient, to say the least. When Claire and Eko discuss the meaning of baptism, she explains that she thinks baptism is what "gets you into heaven." Eko then has the opportunity to explain the actual role of baptism in repentance and its confessional role in identifying the recipient with Jesus as his Liberating King; but Eko seems to have absolutely no grasp of the claims of Christ. He explains to Claire that "when John the Baptist baptized Jesus, the skies opened up and a dove flew down from the sky." He does get this part right; then he adds his interpretation, one far from the orthodox teaching of any church. He says, "This told John something—that he had cleansed this man of all his sins. That he had freed him. Heaven came much later." If Eko's salvation is rooted in his theological understanding, he stands on shaky ground.

Eko seeks out faith with only memories of a brother to guide him and the copy of his brother's Bible Eko discovered in the church after Yemi's death—along with a stick with fragments of verses etched in the hard wood, a mosaic piecing together a picture of his faith. Carved into this "Jesus Stick" (which is what Charlie later mockingly labels it) are biblical references that provide fascinating clues to our mysterious Mr. Eko:

- Acts 4:12—This is the basic tenet of the Christian faith: **"There is no one else who can rescue us, and there is no other name under heaven given to any human by whom we may be rescued."** Of course, anytime the term *salvation* is mentioned on this island, thoughts of rescue come to mind.

- John 3:05—John Locke uses 305 as a compass bearing to find the Flame station. Otherwise, in this biblical passage, Jesus spoke to Nicodemus about being re-created again when he said: **"I tell you the truth, if someone does not experience water and Spirit birth, there's no chance he will make it into God's kingdom."**

- Habakkuk 1:3—The Old Testament prophet Habakkuk wrestles with God over the injustice and violence he has witnessed: **"Why do you force me to see these atrocities? Disaster and violence are raging all around me."** Eko's life is similarly plagued with cruelty and violence, leaving Eko on morally ambiguous ground. Will Eko embrace the God who has allowed such injustice to dominate his life? Can Eko, like Habakkuk, find peace with a powerful God who is large enough to look past circumstance and provide redemptive forgiveness? Habakkuk ends his story, admitting, **"Even if the fig tree does not blossom, and there are no grapes on the vines; if the olive trees fail, and the fields produce no food; if the flocks die far from the fold, and there are no cattle in the stalls; Yet I will still rejoice in the Eternal One! I will rejoice in the God who saves me! The Eternal One, the Lord, is my strength! He has made my feet like the feet of the deer; he allows me to walk on high places." (3:17–19).**

- Titus 3—The New Testament book of Titus speaks of life before and after redemption. We were once disobedient, deceived, and enslaved (the spiritual term for this would be *lost*), but the chapter goes on to describe how believers in Christ are now being renewed by his grace. It also issues a warning against the unrepentant brother who should be cut off from fellowship after being warned twice. Of course, Eko is warned several times to confess before his death. He famously refuses to admit he has sinned when confronted by what appears to be the ghost of his brother

Yemi. Knees to the ground, Eko says, **"Father, I do not confess, for I have not sinned."** Is Eko claiming to be changed and redeemed by a newfound faith he developed on the island or in his years as a faux priest? Or is he proudly claiming to be faultless because his troubled childhood forced him to kill for survival?

- Revelation 5:3—This verse **("No creature of creation in all heaven, on all the earth, or even under the earth could open the scroll or look into its mysteries")** alludes to a scroll that only Christ can open, a book containing a list naming those who are saved. It seems very similar to Jacob's list, in the early episodes, that names which crash survivors must be taken and brought into the Others' community.

Adding to the mystery is the way these particular references are carved. The verse above appears on the stick as "Revelations:3," where the *S* could be the number 5. (Titus:3 is carved on the stick in the same manner.) Revelation 3 is a strict warning to the church in Sardis: "You have a reputation of being alive, but you are dead" (v. 1 NIV). It is also a warning that those who have heard the truth now must repent before it is too late. This is a fitting passage for Eko.

- Psalm 144—This interesting passage reads, **"Eternal One, stretch out an opening in the heavens, and descend. Touch the mountains, and make them smoke. Send forth bolts of lightning, and scatter my enemies. Shoot Your fiery arrows** [remember the flaming arrows raining down on the Losties in season 5?], **and rout the enemy. Reach down from Your high place; save me out of the great waters; rescue me from the grasp of these foreigners who speak only lies and don't have the truth in their deeds"** (vv. 5–8).

- Romans 6:12—This passage reads, **"Don't invite that insufferable tyrant of sin back into your mortal body so you won't become obedient to its destructive desires."** In his forty days of silence (or in the years he has spent as a priest in England and Australia, prior to his arrival on the island), has Eko, perhaps, truly repented?

- HATETH—Along with all these Scriptures, we find one word, *HATETH*, a word used in the Bible to describe Esau: **"I have loved Jacob, but Esau I have hated"** (Malachi 1:2–3 NIV).

- Psalm 23—There is one passage that appropriately stands out above all the others; these six verses may be the most beloved in the Bible.

111

This psalm serves as a companion to the story of the lost sheep told by Jesus:

"The Eternal One is my shepherd, He cares for me always. He provides me rest in rich, green fields beside streams of refreshing water. He soothes my fears; He makes me whole again, steering me off worn, hard paths to roads where truth and righteousness echo His name. Even in the unending shadows of death's darkness, I am not overcome by fear. Because You are with me in those dark moments, near with Your protection and guidance, I am comforted. You spread out a table before me, provisions in the midst of attack from my enemies; You care for all my needs, anointing my head with soothing, fragrant oil, filling my cup again and again with Your grace. Certainly Your faithful protection and loving provision will pursue me where I go, always, everywhere. I will always be with the Eternal One, in Your house forever."

The island's inhabitants seem to be consumed by a power struggle between tribes, and by battles within these tribes, to establish the mantle of leadership. For many seasons it seemed clear that Jack was "the shepherd" with the gifts to lead them, though Sawyer or Locke often challenged him; Eko did not engage in these battles for power and seemed to have no interest in following an earthly shepherd. Did he know something unknown to his companions on this island? He was busy building a church on the island and seemed at peace with his past.

Interestingly, it seems that the actor who plays Eko was a lost child himself . . . in real life. Speaking in his native British accent (which he's never used in any role), he explained to a reporter why leaving ABC's hit show was actually a "joyous" moment. His heightened profile, he said, has opened doors to potential financiers for his long-time pet project: Adewale Akinnuoye-Agbaje plans to direct and star in an autobiographical film he wrote about growing up in foster care and on the tough streets of London. (Africans who immigrated to England in the 1960s and '70s often willingly placed their children in foster care while they adjusted to life in a new country.) In this interview he said, "People that I'd approached [for funding] are now approaching me. It's an opportunity I can't miss." The article goes on to mention his emotional reunion with his parents after he turned eighteen—the lost sheep has been truly found.[1]

Ultimately, Eko's destiny on the island is more perplexing. He denies his need to confess and is consumed by a smoky form that arises from the depths. Is this smoke monster a sovereign and righteous judge that brings justice to evildoers, or an extension of Jacob's adversary, preparing for an apocalyptic climax? The journey toward redemption has been a long, hard road, one that it seems is incomplete. Was Eko written out of this story too soon? Will he return? Or is his ambiguous departure another reminder that this story reflects our real lives? The late actress Gilda Radner summarizes this tension well in her biography as she describes her own life: "I wanted a perfect ending. . . . Now I've learned, the hard way, that some poems don't rhyme, and some stories don't have a clear beginning, middle and end. . . . Life . . . is about not knowing, having to change, taking the moment and making the best of it, without knowing what's going to happen next. Delicious ambiguity."[2] And so it is with Mr. Eko.

John Locke: Patron Saint of the Fatherless

I am clearly more popular than Reagan. I am in my
third term. Where's Reagan? Gone after two! Defeated
by George Bush and Michael Dukakis no less.

—Marion Barry, former mayor of Washington DC

John Locke is hardly the most likable character on *Lost*. Raise your hand if you swear that from the very beginning, the absolute very beginning, you liked Locke; you had no qualms about him at all. Okay, if you're sitting at home or your favorite hipster coffee shop and your hand is held high, go ahead and put it down because (a) it's embarrassing, and (b) you're lying. No one was sure of Locke at first—not the castaways and not the audience. I'll be the first to admit that Locke, as interesting as I think he is, and as glad as I am that he is such a central character on the show, infuriates me much more often than I am drawn to hug him. But at the same time, Locke is heartbreaking and brave and poignantly played. It's just that he's not necessarily the guy to whom we would automatically turn for guidance. How do you say this? It's just that he . . . well, he's a little bit creepy. We would much more readily allow someone like Jack to lead us out of danger and into the promised land. He is smart and handsome, and if you need glasses made from scraps, a tumor removed from your spine, or a quick neonatal examination, Jack is your man. But that doesn't matter; something exists that changes everything, a simple fact that proves our choice to be irrelevant: John Locke is special. He is chosen.

The fact, however, that Locke is special does not make his course any easier. Prior to crashing onto the island, Locke led a dismally lonely and angry existence. For me, these Locke-centric flashback episodes are some of the most painful to watch. Here is a man who has isolated himself, who has given up on the world because of the hurt he has experienced, and while he wants so badly to be special, he cannot accept who he truly is. Oddly enough, the island's man of faith—before he finds the island—is filled with doubt: doubt in others, doubt in himself, doubt in the world—nothing but *doubt*. He was orphaned as a child, and when he finally does get to meet his father, Anthony Cooper, the man turns out to be nothing more than an ailing con man who swindles his son out of a kidney and then takes off, resurfacing only to push Locke out of a window eight stories above the ground. This leaves Locke paralyzed, confined to a wheelchair, and hoping he can make it through life without his "extra" kidney. The bitterness surrounding his broken relationship with his father taints his entire life: he dates a woman whom he loves, but she cannot get over the anger that consumes him; he works an unfulfilling job at a box company because of his debilitating depression that does not allow him to seek other opportunities. We see that he is capable of so much more; we get glimpses of the reality that he is special. But he has locked himself away personally and professionally.

Through the pitfalls and freefalls of it all, John debates with himself about who he will be. He wants so badly to be someone he has no natural inclination to be. As he is growing up, people sense he is gifted, but young Locke does not embrace his gifts and instead spurns them in preference to something . . . more important. Even when Richard Alpert comes to visit the boy Locke in his foster home and presents him with a test composed of the choice between various objects, we get the feeling that John, in choosing the knife, has chosen incorrectly, perhaps in a misconstrued image of himself. In high school, he is asked to attend a prestigious science camp; but Locke fights it, saying that's not who he is—he's an athlete; he likes sports; he is adamantly not a scientist. We look on, wondering what he sees.

Later, as an adult, Locke joins a commune where he meets a young man named Eddie, who seems to look up to John as a father figure. But of course, things are never easy for John, and Eddie is not who he seems; *he* is actually an FBI agent posing as a kid to infiltrate the commune where John lives. In a tense showdown, Eddie refers back to a conversation they had previously about a Native American ritual used to predict one's destiny either as a farmer or a hunter. "You're a good man, John," he says.

"You're a farmer." John, choked by emotion and betrayal, says, "Nope, I was a hunter. I'm a hunter." This scene, like so many of Locke's, is exceedingly tragic. We all know the pain of coming to terms with who you are, with your strengths and weaknesses; and here is a man, well into his adulthood, who still hasn't accepted who he is.

Things change for Locke, however, when one thing happens; and that one thing is, of course, the crash of Oceanic 815. After this, Locke's life is never to be the same. This is the place where Locke literally relearns to walk, and that heralds the beginning of John's journey of self-discovery, his road to understanding what it means to be chosen. But it's not as simple as this: his people belong to someone else. They've already chosen Jack Shephard as their leader. But why? Yes, it's partly because Jack seems a lot more stable and normal than their other options, but the bulk of it is because Locke's people don't know what they're looking for. They've convinced themselves that they are searching for a leader to lead them out of the wilderness, to organize them and get them off the island. They have no idea they need to look for someone to save them.

What a big difference this is too. Pretend you're in a burning building. Would you rather have someone who merely directs you out—or someone who will stop at nothing to save you? You would pick door number two, right? We want someone to save us . . . but only when we really think we need saving. And when we're expecting one thing and given another, we usually fight it because, hey, that's not what we were expecting. So we think that's not what we want or need.

Locke doesn't really fit the profile of the person we expect to not only *lead* his friends but *save* them too. For one thing, he's a little old; we don't expect our saviors to be over forty. And we've already mentioned the creepy part, right? Locke is so intense at times, it's unnerving. At first, because of these obstacles, everyone rejects his leadership. But as Locke becomes more comfortable with his role (a painfully slow process) and the Losties discover the limitations of Jack's leadership, people begin to listen to Locke and follow him. Now at the end of season five, it's undisputed who's running the show: it's Locke (or unLocke, if you will), for good or for ill, dead or alive. His connection with the island is authentic; his dedication to it is religious. His faith is pure and strong. When his bearings are unclear, he banks on what his experiences with the island have been in the past, and moves forward, relying on the knowledge that the island has chosen him. Of course, this isn't to say that Locke's time is void of what plagued him so mercilessly before the plane crash: every now and then we watch doubt debilitate him and challenge his growth. He's able to overcome it, but sometimes it takes a dramatic course of events to refocus him on what's true: Remember when the hatch blew up because of Locke? Remember when the island took away his voice? and the use of his legs? No matter what, though, through all these methods, the island reminds him that he is special. And his time on the island is characterized by reluctance, repentance, and reassurance.

This may seem to be a bit far-fetched, but hear me out: Locke's rise to leadership, his apparent uniqueness, and his possible fulfillment of destiny on the island is reminiscent of Jesus' own messianic role. Jesus, like Locke, had an exceptionally promising childhood, one that hinted at great things to come. There are several key differences, of course, but Jesus, too, had a central event that changed his life forever and secured his place as one chosen by God. By the time Jesus came onto the scene, Jewish messianic expectation had reached near-fanatical proportions. Everyone was anxiously awaiting the arrival of a messiah, a messenger of God who would come set things right in the world. John the Baptist, the wandering, enigmatic prophet, had already come to prepare the way for the coming of someone, he proclaimed, who was more powerful than he, who would baptize people not with water but with the Holy Spirit.

In the first chapter of his gospel, Mark describes the prolific and profound event that would forever alter history (one that is mentioned in *Lost*): the baptism of Jesus. (I've mentioned that the story of Jesus' baptism was a point of discussion for Eko and Claire; but a painting of Jesus being baptized is also hung prominently in Charlie's childhood home.) In Mark's story, John the Baptist baptized Jesus, and as soon as he came out of the water, he saw the heavens being torn open and the Spirit descending to him like a dove. And a voice came from heaven saying:

You are My Son; My beloved One, and I am very pleased with You! (Mark 1:11)

This sealed the deal for Jesus. This apparently simple acknowledgment actually held a significant disclosure: careful students of the Hebrew scriptures would hear a reference to three important passages, three allusions that defined who Jesus was and what his role was to be in the world.

The first refers back to Psalm 2:7, in which the psalmist wrote, "I am telling all of you the truth. I have heard the Eternal One's decree. He said clearly to me, 'You are My Son; today I have become Your Father.'" The rest of the psalm tells of an ultimate king who will come and execute justice. Here, with this allusion, we see two things: first, God the Father claims Jesus as his Son, and second, that Jesus is this king prophesied to come and exact justice in the world, redressing the wrongs in our screwed-up society.

But it doesn't end there. The phrase "I am very pleased

with you" refers to what has become known as the Song of the Suffering Servant, in Isaiah 42. Here Yahweh identifies his servant:

> Behold! My Servant whom I uphold, My Elect One in whom My soul delights! I have put My Spirit upon Him; He will bring forth justice to the Gentiles. He will not cry out, nor raise His voice, nor cause His voice to be heard in the street. A bruised reed He will not break, and smoking flax He will not quench; He will bring forth justice for truth. (1-3, NKJV)

The servant here is someone we would not automatically be expecting. Yahweh says that he won't even break apart a dying twig or put out a candle that's almost burned up. He is gentle, but Yahweh strengthens him, and so he is unstoppable in his mission. The kingdom will be inaugurated through this suffering servant, and by referring back to this song, God declared that Jesus, in coming to bear the sins of the world, is both the ultimate king and the suffering servant. Jesus would have understood this; this is how he would have heard what was said and thus come to view the mission of his life.

The third reference is to the story of Abraham and his son, Isaac. Yahweh instructed Abraham to sacrifice Isaac, and although it was unbearably heartbreaking, Abraham prepared faithfully to obey his Lord. Before the boy could be killed, Yahweh intervened and saved Isaac. However, by affirming that Jesus was his Son, God fulfilled this story, offering his beloved Son as a sacrifice for the world he created. Jesus knew he was the king. He knew that he would suffer and that he would die. He knew all these things, and he went into it anyway . . . because that is what he was called to do by his Father. He came not to lead the people but to turn the world upside down and save them. Jesus also had his doubters. He did not fit their expectations. The Hebrew people were living under Roman occupation and persecution; they needed military might—but Jesus came to rescue them by dying on a Roman cross? It seemed like a plan destined for failure. And at the end of season five, Locke's plan seems even more preposterous. I, for one, am not willing to count him out yet. Rescue is coming.

Sun and Jin: Patron Saints
of Discontented Fishermen

There are two types of fisherman—those who fish for
sport and those who fish for fish.

—Author unknown

What kind of man kills a child's mother before turning the gun on himself—as that child curls up in the corner of the same room? What monster would repeatedly blame and berate a young boy for his mother's death—even though it occurred during childbirth? Who would deceptively offer love and friendship to a lonely soul only to manipulate and then abandon him completely—as he teeters on the edge, both physically and emotionally? Where do you find people this evil? Many names could be used to describe the men who enact these malevolent deeds—scoundrel, villain, fiend, and words much more profane—but on this island, these men are known simply as *father*.

Every man and woman on the island hurts, but as we watch their stories unfold, we learn that the source of their deepest wounds is almost always paternal. Only one character on this island seems to have a loving and honorable father, which may be why he often seems so different from his fellow castaways.

Jin is unlike any of his peers, and the differences run deeper than the fact that he crashed onto the island as the only person who didn't speak English. Jin's story is so contradictory that it pushes the limits of believability, but great acting allows us to accept the reality that a Korean fisherman could become a doorman, gangster, husband, island castaway, ship builder, and Dharma soldier. Go figure! Our favorite Korean husband is known by some on the island (okay, at least by Sawyer) as Mr. Miyagi, Crouching Tiger, Bruce (as in Bruce Lee), Kato, Sulu, Chewie, Papasan, and many other names, but his father named him Jin-Soo-Kwan (권진수/權眞秀). Jin was nurtured in the womb of an insincere and twisted woman, a prostitute with an inclination to manipulate and a total incapacity for maternal love. So Jin's father raises him alone in a very poor village in Korea, providing for him by the arduous and often unrewarding work he learned from his own father—he is a fisherman. This work, however, reflects his love for his son: he labored to offer Jin a better life. But instead of embracing this gift, Jin spends much of his life embarrassed by his father, too ashamed to acknowledge his existence. Jin even goes so far as to claim his father is dead. When Jin marries Sun, his father is not presiding over the event as would be customary for a Korean father—because he was not invited or even notified of his son's nuptials.

Jin's father worked tirelessly to raise his son and offered him unconditional love. Imagine the pain he must feel, then, as Jin tells him that for years he has been lying to friends, family, and even his new wife, claiming his father is dead. Nevertheless, in the face of such blatant rejection, he does not respond in pride or anger. Jesus speaks of a father like this in his own "lost" stories found in Luke 15. An ungrateful and remarkably selfish son disgraces this father, and yet he chooses to love always and forgive at all times. You might notice some similarities between Jin's life and the astonishing story of the lost son told by Jesus.

Once there was this man who had two sons. One day the younger son came to his father and said, "Father, eventually I'm going to inherit my share of your estate. Rather than waiting until you die, I want you to give me my share now." And so the father liquidated assets and divided them. A few days passed and this younger son gathered all his wealth and set off on a journey to a distant land. Once there he wasted everything he owned on wild living. He was broke, a terrible famine struck that land, and he felt desperately hungry and in need. He got a job with one of the locals, who sent him into the fields to feed the pigs. The young man felt so miserably hungry that he wished he could eat the slop the pigs were eating. Nobody gave him anything.

So he had this moment of self-reflection: "What am I doing here? Back home, my father's hired servants have plenty of food. Why am I here starving to death?

I'll get up and return to my father, and I'll say, 'Father, I have done wrong—wrong against God and against you. I have forfeited any right to be treated like your son, but I'm wondering if you'd treat me as one of your hired servants?'" So he got up and returned to his father. The father looked off in the distance and saw the young man returning. He felt compassion for his son and ran out to him, enfolded him in an embrace, and kissed him.

The son said, "Father, I have done a terrible wrong in God's sight and in your sight too. I have forfeited any right to be treated as your son."

But the father turned to his servants and said, "Quick! Bring the best robe we have and put it on him. Put a ring on his finger and shoes on his feet. Go get the fattest calf and butcher it. Let's have a feast and celebrate because my son was dead and is alive again. He was lost and has been found." So they had this huge party. (vv. 11–24)

Our fathers serve as models for what we have the potential of becoming. As such, they shed light on the gifts we possess and warn us of the weaknesses to which we can succumb. While we may glorify movie stars and idolize pretty faces, it is our fathers we mimic—so the role of fatherhood comes with the weight of a great responsibility.

And yet there are so many men who crumple in the face of fatherhood and repeatedly fail their children.

Jesus told the story of the lost son to a crowd who also knew well the pain inflicted by deeply flawed earthly fathers. Yet he spoke of a father (like our heavenly Father) who chose to love in the face of disgrace and forgive despite the careless assaults of a self-absorbed child.

Sun, on the other hand, lives her life as an extension of her imperfect father's will. She adores him publicly and seeks his approval in all things. He is a boss within the Korean mafia who will kill anyone in his way without hesitation; though as a child, Sun doesn't know of her father's murderous background, she does observe and learn that it is perfectly acceptable to use people for her own purposes. Young Sun-Hwa travels through her pampered childhood hand in hand with lies and deceit. When she breaks her father's glass ballerina, she quickly and casually blames the housekeeper, who is promptly dismissed; already Sun has learned how to play every moment to her advantage, seeking to squeeze out the maximum personal gain and discount any potential suffering on the part of others.

Jin falls deeply in love with this woman, but he knows (as he once says), "In a good world . . . she would hate her father, not me." Yet he seeks for a time to become a man like her father—turning his back on the values with which he was raised—in an attempt to maintain Sun in the manner to which she's become accustomed. Meanwhile, does Sun play the role of a patient wife devoted to her husband? No, she spends her days practicing English (in preparation for her escape from a marriage that no longer pleases her) and falling into bed with Jae Lee. Deceit and betrayal have become the lifeblood of this failed union.

Sun and Jin come from complicatedly opposite backgrounds that provide plenty of gunpowder for their explosive union. The sexual and relational tension swirling around them is immense: their marriage is simultaneously repressed and romantic, highbrow and low-class, tender and tense, murderous, adulterous, sterile then fruitful, tragic and yet hopeful. It's been quite a ride over five seasons with this Korean couple, and we've loved every bump and twist of it. At one moment they are madly in love and willing to defy all odds to be together, and moments later they are hiding their deepest secrets from one another. While Bernard and Rose have a sweetly content love, and Desmond and Penny demonstrate a constant, divine love, Sun and Jin are the relationship for the rest of us. Maybe you've never been unfaithful to your spouse or bloodied your hands on behalf of your father-in-law, but Sun and Jin represent the kind of imperfect, struggling love lives most of us possess. The startling beauty in this kind of fraught relationship lies within the characters themselves: their moment-by-moment choices and actions have the power to determine the entire course of their lives. They've earned most of their painful separations with hurtful mistakes that might fatally wound some relationships. But this couple comes fighting back, and when they choose to communicate and to forgive, their reunions are soul satisfying. We keep watching because their love feels familiar. And we wonder, will they be reunited in the end?

Marriage brings out the best and the worst in each of us. As Joyce Brothers often said, "My husband and I have never considered divorce . . . murder sometimes, but never divorce." Even Ghandi claimed, "I first learned the concepts of nonviolence in my marriage."

Two people are joined together as one person but remain weak and vulnerable to their own failures and selfish pursuits. How can they be totally in love at one moment and filled with hatred the next? The Kwon marriage crashes onto the island in its own state of disaster. On the surface it seems that Sun is a loving and subservient wife to her husband, but the appearance could not be further from the truth. The same woman standing quietly behind her man is hiding her hatred, her love affair, her plans to leave, and the truth that he is the reason they are incapable of having children. Jin is angry, explosive, violent, controlling, and seemingly abusive. It is hard to imagine a scenario in which this angry woman and this violent man are able to face their collective demons and emerge to share a life together built on love and mutual trust. But as the lies and deceit are brought out of the darkness and into the light, this marriage experiences a healing that is every bit as miraculous as Locke emerging from a wheelchair. Sun and Jin are in love. Separated by time and blessed with a beautiful baby girl, they remain devoted to one another and determined to be together at any cost. Sun is seeking her husband with the loyalty and passion articulated so beautifully by Ruth in the Old Testament, singing, "Entreat me not to leave thee, or to return from following after thee: for whither thou goest, I will go; and where thou lodgest, I will lodge: thy people shall be my people, and thy God my God" (Ruth 1:16 KJV).

Benjamin Linus:
Patron Saint of Dutiful Tyrants

The one who loves the least controls the relationship.

—Dr. Robert Anthony, American self-help author

In the real world, Ben would be on death row, guilty of mass murder, kidnapping, negligent homicide, torture, conspiracy to commit murder, and possession of the most menacingly creepy grin known to humankind. All of this would easily earn him the death penalty, even in a peace-loving country like Switzerland. But in the convoluted world of *Lost*, Ben is revered and feared, witty and wily. From the moment Ben appeared on-screen (we knew him then as Henry Gale), we were simultaneously drawn to his convincing tall tales and frightened by the menacing look in his bug-eyed stare.

As the story unfolds, we witness perhaps the scariest aspect of Ben: his moral code. He is convinced that he is doing the right thing, keeping all the rules, obeying Jacob, and seeking the greatest good. This, of course, is the terrifying part: Ben seems to be heartless and cruel and swift in his judgments, unswerving in his loyalty to the will of Jacob. If seeking the greatest good and obeying the commands of Jacob require bloodshed, he will not give it a second thought. He is ruthlessly dedicated and dedicatedly ruthless. If the blood that must be shed is from his daughter, Alex, he calls for her execution and does not recoil. He seems to deeply regret her death and feels he should be judged for the role he played in it, but even if he is bluffing to save his own skin (and possibly the skins of those people trapped with him at the time), he does *not* respond with the instincts of a father—who would protect his child at all costs. Ben's perception of familial bonds is deeply broken.

But flash back thirty years and you see that Benjamin Linus was just a quiet, nerdy kid who looked like Harry Potter. Ben was born to Roger and Emily Linus a month too early, causing complications that ultimately resulted in his mother's death. His father, racked by grief and unable to hold a job, signs on with the Dharma Initiative and moves with his young, bespectacled son to the island, becoming a janitor to those changing the world. Ben's relationship with his father is fraught with pain: Roger blames Ben for Emily's death and lashes out explosively and unpredictably. He hurls words like stones at his son, who inevitably learns to walk the line between bitterly fragile and quietly angry.

Ben lives in the Dharma community but attaches to no one, and this loneliness, this feeling of not belonging, festers inside him. As an adult, Ben sums up his aloneness by quoting from John Steinbeck's *Of Mice and Men*: "A guy goes nuts if he ain't got nobody. Don't make no difference who the guy is, long's he's with you. I tell ya, I tell ya, a guy gets too lonely and he gets sick."

Dharmaville is hardly utopia, but it is certainly not hell either. You work, eat, dance, swim, play board games and volleyball. How does a young boy grow up in a small community like this and fail to form the kinds of bonds that prevent him from poisoning the entire village?

Ben's only childhood friend is a sweet-faced girl named Annie, who immediately takes Ben under her wing on the island. She presents him with his sole birthday gift: two wooden doll versions of themselves. Ben gets the Annie doll, and Annie gets the Ben doll; this way, she tells him, they will never be apart. This appears to be Ben's only significant human relationship, and he often appears awkward and tongue-tied even in her presence.

He knows even from the beginning that although he is a part of the Dharma community, he does not belong to them. He is an outsider; he feels this instinctively. These awkward, lonely childhood years teach him to bide his time, to persevere. Ultimately Ben kills his father and makes the Hostiles' (a.k.a. Others) purge of the Dharma Initiative possible, securing his place in the Hostiles' fold. Years later he explains to John Locke that, while the Dharma folks were his people, "they couldn't even coexist with the island's original inhabitants . . . and when it became clear that one side had to be purged, I did what I had to do." Ben knows how to play the game. He progresses from a tongue-tied youth to a masterful manipulator of words. He uses language the way Sayid uses his fists, and he does it all for the island—for Jacob.

Ben Linus is obedient, at least to the letter of the law, if not the spirit of it. He places his complete faith in Jacob and the island and focuses on doing the right thing, believing that his obedience gives him special rights. But as Paul the apostle says,

> What if I speak in the most elegant languages of people or in the exotic languages of the heavenly messengers, but I live without love? Well then, anything I say is like the clanging of brass or a crashing cymbal. What if I have the gift of prophecy, am blessed with knowledge and insight to all the mysteries, or what if my faith is strong enough to scoop a mountain from its bedrock, yet I live without love? If so, I am nothing. I could give all that I have to feed the poor, I could surrender my body to be burned as a martyr, [that I may brag,] but if I do not live in love, I gain nothing by my selfless acts."
> (1 Corinthians 13:1–3)

(That scooping a mountain from its bedrock phrase sounds a bit like moving an island, huh?)

Ben has it all, at least on one level: a purpose, a steadfast faith in his belief system, a beautiful daughter, a respected place of leadership in his community, power, wealth, and a life filled with adventure. But love is absent, and it is love that illuminates the rest of life with purpose and meaning. Without it, life becomes a set of rules and lists that we must complete. Ben follows the rules and looks down in anger on everyone else who does not comply. The first time John Locke demands to see Jacob, Ben is furious, appalled that his position as Jacob's right-hand man is being challenged. He is terrified that perhaps Jacob will be angry with him, or worse yet, replace him with this disrespectful and sacrilegious heretic. Locke doesn't believe Jacob truly exists, to Ben's bewilderment, and Ben snobbishly and angrily says to John, "I'm sorry that you're too limited to see." Going to visit Jacob takes on an Old Testament sort of feel: tiptoeing around an explosive deity who values protocol and ritual over the true exploration of faith. And when Jacob *does* speak to Locke, Ben is horrified and jealous. He is the one who deserves to hear Jacob speak; he is the one who has sacrificed so much of himself (and others) to Jacob.

This anger finally explodes when Ben meets Jacob for the first time face-to-face. Ben rages against him, saying, "So now, after all this time, you've decided to stop ignoring me. Thirty-five years I lived on this island, and all I ever heard was your name over and over. Richard would bring me your instructions—all those slips of paper, all those *lists*—and I never questioned anything. I did as I was told. But when I dared to ask to see you myself, I was told, 'You have to wait. You have to be patient.' But when he [John] asked to see you? He gets marched straight up here as if he was Moses. So . . . why him? Hmm? What was it that was so wrong with me? What about me?"

Sound familiar? In Jesus' own "lost" narrative, we see a character who sounds a great deal like Ben Linus. The family, neighbors, servants, and friends begin a massive celebration. They are filled with joy because the lost son has been found. But one person in the story does not see this as a cause for celebration. The gospel of Luke tells us:

Now the man's older son was still out in the fields working. He came home at the end of the day and heard music and dancing. He called one of the servants and asked what was going on. The servant said, "Your brother has returned, and your father has butchered the fattest calf to celebrate his safe return."

The older brother got really angry and refused to come inside, so his father came out and pleaded with him to join the celebration. But he argued back, "Listen, all these years I've worked hard for you. I've never disobeyed one of your orders. But how many times have you even given me a little goat to roast for a party with my friends? Not once! This is not fair! So this son of yours comes, this wasteful delinquent who has spent your hard-earned wealth on loose women, and what do you do? You butcher the fattest calf from our herd!"

The father replied, "My son, you are always with me, and all I have is yours. Isn't it right to join in the celebration and be happy? This is your brother we're talking about. He was dead and is alive again; he was lost and is found again!" (15:25–32)

Jesus never concluded the story of the older son in Luke 15. We see the father lovingly pursue him as his rage explodes, but we never find out if the father's expression of unconditional love changed him too. The story is yet to unfold with Ben as well. Will he get another chance at redemption? Will he repent of his role in his daughter's death, mourn, and finally have a chance to heal? He seems to have a heart of stone, but harder hearts have been melted in the presence of the divine.

We may never know how the older son responded, or how Benjamin Linus evolves, but we are able to discover how our own stories will end. We see ourselves in the older brother and in Ben when we believe that we deserve what we have, that somehow we have earned status by doing the right thing. Perhaps we make the same mistake Ben made in Jacob's home when he put himself at the center of the story. Of course, Ben has no idea that John

Locke isn't merely himself as he confronts Jacob. Ben's plaintive cry, "What about me?" seems childish in light of the sabotage Jacob's old nemesis, the Man in Black, has underway. But Ben is relying on karma (you reap what you sow)—if he's been ruthlessly faithful to Jacob, Jacob should reward him faithfully. But life on *Lost* is a lot like real life, and karma just doesn't pan out. We do not get what we deserve. Fortunately, we receive grace instead. Bono explains it this way:

> It's a mind-blowing concept that the God who created the universe might be looking for company, a real relationship with people, but the thing that keeps me on my knees is the difference between grace and karma. Grace defies reason and logic. Love interrupts, if you like, the consequences of your actions, which in my case is very good news indeed, because I have received much more than I deserve.[1]

The moment we shift our focus from entitlement (getting what we deserve) to grace (celebrating the reality that we have received forgiveness and love that we could never earn and do not deserve), we become less like the older brother and are welcomed to a great feast at the Father's table.

Jacob: Patron Saint of Fathers

Come mothers and fathers throughout the land, and don't criticize what you can't understand.

—Bob Dylan, American singer-songwriter

According to biblical accounts, Jacob is the blessed son of Isaac and father to a nation known as Israel. But according to J. J. Abrams, our latter-day Jacob is a mysterious force, an enigmatic leader who skillfully weaves at the looms of destiny and thread, expertly pulls fish from the sea, and still has time to ponder the writings of the greatest storyteller from the American South, Flannery O'Connor. So while we know that Jacob harbors some odd sort of power and that he has a penchant for comically macabre American literature, our real knowledge of this figure falls short (considering we only just *saw* the guy in the season five finale.) Who is he exactly? A god? A prophet? Or just a man who prefers living in the shadow of a statue to paying the exorbitant rent charged in most coastal areas?

Obviously, Jacob's personality is so enigmatic that we cannot offer many solid facts regarding his true purpose in the show. However, there are a few clear facts about Jacob thus far:

1. Jacob has both an adversary and a loyal following.

The biblical Jacob was domestically gifted and used food as a weapon against his brother, Esau, in order to steal his birthright; his brother later vowed to kill him, and he was forced to seek sanctuary in a foreign land near ancient Egypt. Ultimately, he fathered a large family in exile that grew into the nation of Israel.

Similarly, the Jacob of the island is both gifted and blighted: we know that he possesses strengths akin to his biblical predecessor because we see him masterfully weave great tapestries and baskets to trap fish. And as far as enemies go, island Jacob is threatened by his adversary on a beach sometime prior to the nineteenth century. Island Jacob offers this man food, and the man not only refuses but also vows to find a way, a "loophole," he says, through which he will finally kill Jacob. Jacob then seeks sanctuary in the hidden vault of an ancient Egyptian statue, where he quietly leads the people of the group he has founded, whom we know as the Others.

These parallels provide many clues that are likely to guide the story. Think about the relationships this way: if Israel is God's chosen people, are the Others God's chosen people as well? The children of Jacob were led into Egypt, where they became slaves and their children were slaughtered at birth; our island inhabitants are also strangers in a strange land, reliving cycles of violence for who knows how long. They are enslaved, in a sense, in this new home from which there is no escape, and they are subject to the loss of their children because all women who become pregnant on the island die before they are able to give birth. God sent Moses to lead his people out of slavery in Egypt into a land he promised them; and in this we begin to see many parallels between the life of Moses and the story unfolding on *Lost*. We see elements of Moses through the leadership of Locke. Biblically, Moses is hesitant to accept his role as leader; he questions himself as God's choice to lead his people out of slavery. In Exodus 3:11, we are told, "Moses did not understand how he could be the one to fulfill such a destiny." Moses did not fit the definition of *special* in any sense of the word other than this: Moses was chosen, and because he was chosen, he was special. His story is not about qualifications and credentials—what makes Moses special is the promise that God will be with him. God offers Moses his personal name, "I AM," and this, this name, simply and profoundly signifies his unyielding commitment.

Locke's story unfolds similarly. Throughout the series we watch as Locke painstakingly fights to be special. We watch him struggle with what appears to be ordinariness and then, conversely, with his role as chosen leader; we watch him hesitate and doubt his ability to serve the island, or Jacob. But Jacob is faithful to Locke. He has spoken to Locke (he has even touched him). He is committed to Locke. Even Ben Linus expresses to Jacob his disgust that Locke is given a private meeting in the inner sanctum of Jacob's dwelling as if he were Moses himself. Is John Locke a Moses for the island? Is someone coming to rescue God's people from captivity, violence, oppression, and the deep grief of perpetually grieving the dying mothers-to-be? If seasons one through five tell the story of the island, its inhabitants (the descendants of Adam and Eve), and where they have come from, much like Genesis, then I believe that season six will be the story of the exodus. Perhaps they won't all physically escape from the island, but they will all be "delivered" from being spiritually and emotionally "lost" slaves.

2. Jacob has not aged in the last two hundred years (at least), and he is the force keeping Richard Alpert similarly youthful.

Jacob possesses mystical powers; and while (surprise, surprise) what, exactly, these powers entail is unclear, we can discern one thing: Jacob is, good or bad, a commanding and powerful force. He is ageless, or at least retains a youthful physical mien, and, as we learned in season five, he has granted Richard Alpert the same cool party trick. Although we can't be absolutely sure where or how he got this ability, we can venture that it is because of his intrinsic connection to the island. Jacob seems like a part of the island: he is the island's megaphone, its prophet, and its voice. It is widely understood that Jacob speaks on behalf of the island, and at times, his connection to it makes him almost interchangeable with it. He is a force that generally goes unquestioned, an authority representative of an unnatural union with the terrene, the human manifestation of the earth.

Jacob also has the power to heal. In season three, Juliet, a brilliant fertility specialist who has left her home in Miami to join the Others, becomes a principal player in the goings-on of the island. She leaves behind a sister, Rachel, stricken with cancer. Juliet, having been dishonestly told that she would be able to leave the island eventually, is held captive by Ben Linus, bound by this one condition: if she leaves, her sister's health will deteriorate. If she stays, however, Ben promises that Jacob will personally attend Rachel's case; that is, if Juliet will have faith in Jacob's power, Rachel will be cured. Juliet is unable to leave and soon learns that Rachel's cancer is in remission, seemingly vanished.

Two seasons later we see the restorative power of Jacob again, this time with Ben Linus himself. After being shot by a time-traveling Sayid, young Ben is on the precipice of death, and, while the back-in-time-castaways-turned-Dharma-Initiative-members all know who the young bespectacled Ben becomes, Kate cannot bring herself to allow a child, even "evil" Ben, to die. She enlists the help of Juliet, who knows that the Others may be able to fix Ben. Sure enough, Richard confirms that Jacob could heal Ben, but with one serious caveat: if he takes Ben, "he will never be the same again . . . his innocence will be lost." Despite this warning, Kate and Sawyer, who is helping her, leave Ben with the Others, and Ben is healed, allowing whatever happened to happen.

There are two other cases of miraculous healings on the island. One, of course, is John Locke, who, wheelchair-bound before the crash, regains his ability to walk after landing on the island. Ben Linus (all grown up) explains to Locke that this is the work of the island and, more importantly, its will: "The island wanted me sick. It wanted you well. My time is over." The island healed John in order to usher in his time of leadership (and it gave Ben cancer as a lovely parting gift). The second character healed is Rose, whose cancer seems to go into remission when she arrives on the island—and while she is only a secondary, albeit popular, character, her condition serves as another testimony to the island's restorative power. But these two scenarios prompt a question: who or what is truly in charge? Is it Jacob, or is it the island? Can they both cure people, or does Jacob do the island's bidding? Or is the island, as we mentioned earlier, the natural manifestation of Jacob's power?

3. Jacob makes lists and, historically, his people obey.

Throughout the *Lost* story, the name of Jacob is used to evoke fear and obedience. To believe in Jacob is to obey him. He is the absolute authority on the island. As Ben says, "We all answer to someone." And that someone, for everyone, is Jacob. In a flashback to the 1970s, when Richard Alpert is advised to tell the leaders Charles and Ellie his plans, he responds that he doesn't answer to them, only to Jacob. Later Ben defaults to that same rationale: after he has stolen baby Alex from her mother, Rousseau, then-leader Widmore chastises him for disobeying Jacob by leaving Rousseau alive. Widmore commands Ben to kill the infant, claiming that it is the will of Jacob. Ben, however, retorts that if it were truly the will of Jacob, Widmore would be able to kill the baby himself. Jacob's ways are mysterious, and his true adherents defy those who use his name merely to justify their own selfish actions.

Jacob himself, however, is a little harder to defy. Ben describes him as unforgiving and fairly callous. The very mention of him is ominous. He is somehow connected to

Room 23, the brainwashing facility in which Karl is held. (Walt was also held here.) One of the screens flashes Jacob's name, and when Karl escapes, he mutters, barely conscious, "God loves you as he loved Jacob," the words he'd seen on the screen. Jacob seems ancient, almost primeval. In season three, Locke pays a visit to Jacob's cabin, and even this trek communicates an Old Testament sort of feel: this is a power to cautiously tip-toe around, an explosive deity who values protocol and rewards ritual over the exploration of faith. He keeps a record of those people whom he considers good, people whom he wants to bring into the Others' camp. The Others are fanatical in their attempts to achieve this. "Who are we," Ben asks, "to argue with who's on the list?"

4. Jacob visits the Losties at times in their lives when they need him most, but he does not believe he is intended to control destinies; instead, it is up to each person to choose his or her own path.

Much like the father in Jesus' story of the lost son, Jacob pursues his children. When young Kate ventures off the straight and narrow to steal a New Kids on the Block lunch box, who is there to pay for her infraction and nudge her back on the path? Jacob. Who speaks a profound blessing (in perfect Korean, no less) over Sun and Jin as they embark on a marital life that will be filled with tribulation? Jacob. When Hurley emerges from prison, scared, confused, and feeling both insane and cursed, who calls him back into community and enlightens him to the reality that he is not cursed, but actually blessed? Jacob. As Jack melts down during a critical moment in surgery and must face both his insecurities and misguided need to blame his father, who is there to pull his candy bar from the machine and offer a wise word? You guessed it: Jacob. In the moment with Jack, he offers a little insight into his participation in the stories that pull us all together, referring to much more than a candy bar dangling on a ledge in a caged vending machine. He explains that sometimes things "just need a little push."

After John Locke free-falls from fatal heights, it is Jacob who touches him and seems to breathe life into his crushed frame. But although he is present in the scene, Jacob stands idle as Sayid's love, Nadia, is killed by a hit-and-run driver. What is Jacob doing? One moment he is healing, and in another he is an accomplice to murder in his passivity. Is he orchestrating all these events, or simply adding a nudge here and there?

If we take Jacob at his word, we all possess the power to choose. As Ben's sense of thwarted entitlement and anger turns to murderous rage, Jacob reminds him, "Benjamin . . .

whatever he's told you, I want you to understand one thing. You have a choice. You can do what he asked, or you can go, leave us to discuss our . . . issues." But Ben does not see the events to follow as a choice. Perhaps his course of action was orchestrated long ago, and he was intended and expected to fulfill his role.

So given all the known facts, we are left to ponder the similarities this enigmatic character shares with God himself—or to the Jacob character of the Bible, who also loved a son named Benjamin. Jacob's youngest son was born to his beloved wife Rachel, and when he blessed Benjamin in Genesis, he described him as a "ravenous wolf; in the morning he shall devour the prey, and at night he shall divide the spoil" (49:27, NKJV). There may be something in a name.

5. Jacob believes history is moving toward something more connected and meaningful than what lies in the past.

Depending on where you stand, the future appears brighter than the present, or looks dark and foreboding instead. Jacob's adversary, a man clothed in black, announces his disgust at the sight of a boat advancing slowly toward the island. He believes Jacob has brought these guests to the island and says, "They come. They fight. They destroy.

They corrupt. It always ends the same." But Jacob differs, saying, "It only ends once. Anything that happens before that is just progress." This idea alludes, perhaps, to two similar veins of thought. First, we could take this statement as a possible reference to the development of the Jewish perspective on apocalyptic eschatology. Before Judaism, people saw the world unfolding in a cyclical way; that is, everything moved circularly, in the way the seasons do: spring, summer, autumn, winter, endlessly repeating. There was not necessarily an end in sight. But when Judaism developed, so did a new mind-set regarding apocalyptic thought. Suddenly our timeline shifted from cyclical to linear, making our time on the earth simply one point in the unfolding of history. In *Lost*, of course, Jacob's adversary embodies the former viewpoint, while the latter viewpoint is characterized by Jacob, with his assertion that we are moving toward an end, that we are slowly progressing down a linear timeline.

The other possible reference point for this conversation is the worldview touted by French philosopher Pierre Teilhard de Chardin. Teilhard purported that the world is moving toward a state of deep connection and collective thought. All things are bending toward one another and changing as they come together; machines become more like man, and man more like machines. Darkness is turning to light and light to darkness. And the ultimate connection (or convergence) is with God. Essentially the philosophy can be described as "Everything that rises must converge," a phrase Teilhard uses in his book *The Future of Man*. It is also the title of a book of short stories by Flannery O'Connor—the very book Jacob is reading as he awaits the arrival of John Locke, who was pushed from an eighth-story window.

As participants in the epic story we know as *Lost*, we struggle to imagine an approaching end. It feels apocalyptic, yet it is hard to imagine an appropriate ending or the finality of accepting that the coming years will not bring another season of episodes that both tease and satisfy. D. H. Lawrence once described a similar tension shared by the believers charged with the sacred task of compiling the Christian biblical canon. He said,

> We can understand that the Fathers of the Church in the East wanted Apocalypse left out of the New Testament. But like Judas among the disciples, it was inevitable that it should be included. The Apocalypse is the feet of clay to the grand Christian image. And down crashes the image, on the weakness of these very feet.

There is Jesus—but there is also John the Divine. There is Christian love—and there is Christian envy. The former would 'save' the world—the latter will never be satisfied till it has destroyed the world. They are two sides of the same medal.[1]

Jacob dwells in these feet of clay, and we are left to await a climax to this story, wondering how love might prevail.

16

The Lovers:
Desmond Hume and Penelope Widmore

What is love?

—Howard Jones/William Bryant (1983)

The true motives of every castaway and tribe connected to this island are questionable. And we relish the suspicions: we suspect Ben Linus and Charles Widmore may be exploiting the magical properties of the island for their own self-aggrandizement and financial gain. Locke may be attempting to prove he is truly special, while Jack may be feeding his pathological savior complex by fixing every lost cause. Yet there is one man who stands alone, pursuing his fate wholly untainted, motivated solely by love: Desmond Hume. Why does he challenge Charles Widmore and sail the globe against all odds, spend years in an isolated hatch pressing the same button, and repeatedly risk his life to escape the island? There is one answer: to be reunited with Penelope Widmore, the love of his life.

If you didn't cry in season four's episode "The Constant," something is wrong with you; you were either distracted or, worse, it is possible you have no soul. No matter how stiff your upper lip, this kind of love and self-sacrifice brings out the romantic in each of us. For those who haven't memorized the names of all 103 episodes, this is the one in which Desmond takes a page from Billy

Pilgrim's book and becomes unfettered to time. According to *Lost*'s physicist, Daniel Faraday, in order to survive this nonchronological bouncing around, a time traveler must establish a constant—someone who plays a significant role in both his past and present life. This constant figure keeps his mind grounded, and keeps his brain from dripping out of his nose. Desmond's constant is Penny, the woman he loves—and daughter of Other-leader-turned-big-time-bad-guy, Charles Widmore. The episode ends with a poignantly weepy phone call between Desmond and Penny as the two profess their love for one another despite being separated by thousands of miles and many years. They've chosen to believe love will bring them back together, regardless of all the evidence to the contrary.

Desmond and Penelope are the truest example of love on *Lost* (aside from Rose and Bernard), and while they share limited screen time together, their story makes a profound statement about what love really is. Throughout the entire series thus far, we've been shown, through the romantic entanglements of these characters, which qualities of a relationship to embrace and which to reject. We get to see the entire course of Desmond and Penny's time together: We watch as he gets scared, runs away, and then repents. We watch as Penny pursues, is hurt, reacts angrily, and then forgives. We know they're on their way to figuring out this whole love thing . . . but they aren't quite there yet. We see a reflection of our own mistakes in their starry-eyed and broken journeys, and—as *we* often do—they hurt those they love the most, longing for intimacy and yet deathly afraid of it. Like Penny and Des, we want to love selflessly, but we fear rejection and impulsively rebuff true love.

Perhaps the most compelling part of Desmond and Penny's relationship is how widely applicable their story is; it is not limited to romantic love but instead recalls the scope and magnitude of love in general. And while it may seem a bit far-fetched, we can examine the qualities of their love for one another and apply it to how we view God and his unbelievable, unquantifiable, unstoppable love for us.

We meet Penny at the end of her relationship with Desmond, or what seems to be the end of their relationship. Desmond has just turned the key in the hatch, releasing the electromagnetic energy of the island, imploding the hatch, and, as Hurley later describes it, this energy turns the sky purple. This profound event sends Desmond, oddly enough, back in time and across the world, where he wakes up in the flat he shares with Penny, with his memories of the island intact. He is overjoyed to see her, but his elation quickly flounders as he succumbs to his monumental self-doubt. He tells Penelope, "I can't. I can't look after you . . . you deserve better." Penny replies, heartbroken and angry, "I know what I deserve. I choose you . . . If you don't want this, don't make it about what I do or don't deserve. Have the decency to admit that you're doing this because you're a coward." What's the real problem here? Penny is right: it's not an issue with her; rather it's about Desmond and his self-perception and his inability to reconcile his idea of what Penny deserves with the person he is. He cannot understand love given without merit, and it is clear to him that Penny's is a love he does not deserve. Her love is true and selfless: Desmond may be a coward. He may not have a job. But she loves him all the same.

It's the same with God's love, only on an exponentially grander scale. God's love is unconditional. We can't do anything to stop God from loving us; he doesn't change his mind, nor does he evaluate our actions and then love us accordingly. If he did, he would be selfish with his love, unable to bestow it upon any of his creation. Instead, because his love is perfect and without parameters, he grants it freely and happily. Take Israel, for example. In the Old Testament, Israel was a rebellious nation of people who got into all kinds of trouble—but God loved them anyway. There was nothing humanly possible they could have done to *make* God love them. He just chose them. That's all it took. God deserves better than what we have to offer, but he chooses us. And he gladly accepts us. Through the sacrifice of Jesus, God holds us—as surely as Penny redeemed Desmond.

Like Desmond, we often refuse to accept this free love

as a gift that cannot be earned, and so we swing between two extremes. We either try to earn that love with grand displays that will inevitably leave us in the same position as the ever-determined Desmond—shipwrecked and alone—or we wallow in self-pity, stating the obvious—that we have been given more than we deserve. The third path is a more fulfilling and beautiful way to live; in it, we simply celebrate the remarkable blessing that has been given to us and see it as a reason to share our love and forgiveness freely as well.

In 1 Corinthians 13, Paul wrote about this unique sort of love, and he broke it down in a way that makes this complex idea of eternal, undeserved love a bit more comprehensible. He didn't offer a greeting-card expression of love or even a textbook definition; instead he used simple examples that let us glimpse what love looks like in an active, pure form. In other words, he told us exactly what love—both divine and neighborly—does and does not do. "Love," he wrote, "is patient; love is kind. Love isn't envious, doesn't boast, brag, or strut about. There's no arrogance in love; it's never rude, crude, or indecent—it's not self-absorbed. Love isn't easily upset. Love doesn't tally wrongs or celebrate injustice, but truth—yes, truth—is love's delight!" (vv. 4–6).

Paul makes it clear for us: if the love we experience or the love we give is impatient, if it's unkind, then somewhere down the line we've gotten mixed up. We've made a mistake . . . because this love, this patient, kind, content, selfless love, is the love God embodies, and therefore is the love we must learn to receive from him and then give to others.

Look at Desmond and Penelope in light of these verses. They reflect this kind of transcendent love. Desmond inexplicably breaks up with Penny, runs away, and acts like a selfish moron. But Penelope is patient: she waits and she forgives. First, of course, she's hurt, and that pain shows itself as anger. When Desmond tries to call her and ask for help, she hangs up on him. This hardly seems a loving thing to do, and seems even farther away from how we would expect our heavenly Father to react. Would God ignore us if we asked him for help? No. But does he hurt when we run away from him? Yes.

In fact, God was angry when Israel turned her back on him. But he forgave her; this is part of God's love for us. He pursued Israel the way the biblical prophet Hosea pursued his wife, Gomer. God commanded Hosea to marry a prostitute. Obedient, Hosea found himself married with children to a woman he loved. In far from a happy ending, however, Gomer cheated on Hosea over and over; she even returned to her old job. (It would be like Julia Roberts leaving Richard Gere at the end of *Pretty Woman* to turn tricks on the grimy street.) Then God commanded Hosea to track Gomer down and bring her home, to woo her back into love with him. Hosea was deeply wounded as a man and husband, but he did it. Why would God ask a man to endure all that? He wanted a real-life example of how his heart had been broken by Israel's unfaithfulness. This God we pray to and believe in has actual feelings; he hurts like a man betrayed by his own wife, because his love is so great for us all. And this is how he pursues us, even when our backs are belligerently turned to him. No matter what we've done, it's never too late—because in his perfect love there is always forgiveness.

By the time of their Christmas Eve phone call in "The Constant," Desmond's slate is wiped clean—Penny has forgiven the wrongs Desmond committed and is simply overjoyed to hear that he is not only alive but still enamored with her. Throughout everything, Penny remains in Desmond's corner, and he in hers. To be so confidently in love with one another is beautiful and transcendent, allowing us to peek into the very heart of God.

The last part of 1 Corinthians 13 is profound in its simple truth and perfectly summarizes Penny and Desmond's relationship: Love, Paul wrote, "puts up with anything and everything that comes along; it trusts, hopes, and endures no matter what. Love will never become obsolete" (vv. 7–8). This is the love Penny and Desmond have for one another and, more importantly and perfectly, the love our Father has for us. Love survives hardship; it survives doubt and pain and loneliness. It bears *everything*, Paul said; it believes *everything*—there's no stranded-on-a-deserted-magical-island clause. It trumps everything we could throw at it. And doesn't it make sense now, in light of this assertion, that Desmond and Penny could be apart for years and still manage to hold on to that love for one another? Desmond keeps a photo of Penelope with him at all times; his faith that it's not over, his belief that their love is real, burns an image inside him that he holds with him. He can't see her, but he knows she's real and that she is somewhere suffering the same pain he feels at their separation.

This is faith: to feel the truth but not see it directly . . . and still remain filled with hope. It's the same for us in the real world. We are lost sometimes—there's no getting around that painful fact—but through it all we can count on this love that hopes all things, that endures all things. This hope, this love, manifests itself in our faith in a loving God.

The idea of putting up "with anything and everything" inspires an image of pursuit, an element central to the story of Desmond and Penny. For the three years Desmond is missing, Penny has relentlessly pursued him. Nothing dissuades her from dropping everything to find

Desmond—not even Desmond himself, who runs away in the first place because he's scared of the implications of accepting and returning her love. It's only when he has lost her that he realizes how transforming love can be. This separation proves to Desmond that true love is unmerited, inexplicable, and fiercely magnetic. He finally sees that he does not, and indeed cannot, earn Penny's love. The time and years that come between them allow Penelope to demonstrate how relentless love can be. Desmond tells Charlie, "I tried to run away from her but she tracked me down . . . she never gave up. She's spent the last three years looking for me."

Remember Jesus' own lost stories? He tells about a woman losing her wedding coin, then about a man who loses one sheep. In each story, the person who has lost something of value drops everything to track it down—because love never gives up, because that coin, that sheep, is profoundly important to the person it belongs to. This is how Penny feels about Desmond; this is how God feels about us. If we end up missing, God desires one thing more than anything else: to be reunited with the person he loves. To ensure this divine reunion, he pursues us with the unstoppable force of his love. Nothing can stand in his way! Paul gave the Romans a graphic example of this when he wrote, "For I have every confidence that nothing—not death, life, heavenly messengers, dark spirits, the present, the future, spiritual powers, height, depth, nor any created thing—can disconnect us from the love of God that came to us in Jesus, our Lord and Liberating King" (Romans 8:38–39). Nothing can stand between us and the love of the living God: not our fear or reluctance, not the disapproval of others, nothing. And even then, for as long as it takes for us to accept it, his love will bear all things, believe all things, hope all things, and endure all things. Love never fails.

Daniel Faraday:
Patron Saint of Mystic Scientists

The least movement is of importance to all nature.
The entire ocean is affected by a pebble.

—Blaise Pascal, French mathematician,
physicist, and philosopher (1623–1662)

Daniel Faraday is (or was, depending on how certain you are about the reality of his death at the hand of his young mother in the fifth season) an exceptional man by anyone's standards; in fact, I would wager to say his mother believes he is smarter than Einstein. We watch him as a young boy breezing through Frédéric Chopin's Fantaisie-Impromptu in C-sharp minor, one of Chopin's most rhythmically challenging pieces. His mother, however, boldly declares that he must stop wasting his time playing piano because it only serves as a distraction to his true gift. His true gift? You mean piano, isn't it? With a single question she makes her point: "How many clicks," she asks, "have you heard the metronome make since you started playing?" Without pause, young Daniel answers precisely: there were 864 clicks. His mother explains that his real gift, the one that matters, is his mind, "a mind that is meant for science, mathematics. And it's my job to keep you on your path. So . . . unfortunately, there's no more time." In that moment she zeroes in on what she understands to be Daniel's entire purpose in the world. His mind is his destiny, a special gift, she says, that must be nurtured.

And his gift is nurtured indeed. Daniel's academic career takes him through a doctoral program at Oxford and lands him a job as professor at his alma mater, where he begins his own unauthorized research, studying time travel and even building a machine that allows the subject's mind to "travel" while the body stays put. (And all this research is on Charles Widmore's dollar.) Despite the barrier his eccentricities build between himself and his colleagues, Daniel quickly gains notoriety as a brilliant, albeit odd, addition to academia.

Daniel longs to leave the laboratory and pursue a normal life, but his deep desire to please his mother and the weight of his gift do not allow it. In fact, he risks the life of his girlfriend for the sake of his research. But his mother may be right; Daniel is not like the rest of us. We mere mortals likely fill our personal journals with doodles, lists, and fragmented thoughts or the occasional attempt at poetry, but when we (and a soon-to-be die-hard believer, Jack Shephard) have the chance to peer into the journal of Daniel Faraday, we see indecipherable jargon: the Lorentz invariance, the Kerr metric, and the Eddington-Finkelstein coordinates. You know, just your everyday scientist street talk. (Now that I think about it, I will send a free bag of fair-trade coffee to any person reading this book who knows what these words refer to without the use of Wikipedia. I am serious. Go for it.) As you might imagine, all these terms relate to the general theory of relativity and describe properties of space-time. It was Albert Einstein who took the Newtonian understanding of space and time as two separate entities and linked them together as one single fabric, hence known as space-time. This linkage is the basis of Faraday's understanding of what makes time travel possible. He describes this unit of space-time as a record album, saying, "Think of the island like a record spinning on a turntable . . . only now, that record is skipping. Whatever Ben Linus did down at the Orchid station . . . I think . . . it may have . . . dislodged us." In its simplest form, then, time travel can be described as being dislodged from the continuous blanket of space-time.

Einstein's work led us all out of a Newtonian world—in which we believed the world was governed by simple laws of gravity—into a much more mysterious world of quantum mechanics, forcing us to embrace mystery and endless possibilities that, at times, break Newton's laws. This world of quantum physics began in 1838 when Michael Faraday, our hero's namesake, discovered that streams of electrons could be observed in vacuum tubes. Michael Faraday's work in the 1800s set the sciences on a path that allows us to look at increasingly smaller units of matter. There are inherent risks at summarizing centuries of scientific research, but, simply put, the closer we look at matter, the more awe-inspiring and mysterious it becomes. Science often evokes one of two responses from regular folks who are not studying physics, say, or who don't as a habit read scientific journals or dream of working for NASA:

1. **Awe and wonder**. An appreciation of natural science creates a profound sense of wonder about the natural order, which can lead to a healthy posture of engagement with scientific ideas or a complete capitulation to anything the latest research suggests.

2. **Fear and anger**. The latest scientific findings often threaten the status quo, and many people find themselves defending false premises with their lives. It might be quantum physics, evolution, or the assertion that the earth is round; what's important is that all people, but especially people of faith, come to realize that they have no reason to fear an honest dialogue with the sciences. It is, after all, the pursuit of truth. And you know what Jesus had to say about the truth: it *will* set you free.

Your understanding of Einstein's general theory of relativity, quantum physics, or time travel might be comparable to Hurley's own limited scientific cognizance. Any familiarity he has with the subject comes from comic books and the *Back to the Future* films. When it becomes clear that his jaunt backwards in time could have an effect on the future, he leans on a logic that only survives scrutiny in Hollywood. As he carefully watches to see if he is slowly disappearing, Hurley defends his logic to Miles: "It is like *Back to the Future*, man. We came back in time to the island and changed stuff. So if little Ben dies, he'll never grow up to be big Ben, who's the one who made us come back here in the first place. Which means we can't be here. And therefore, dude? We don't exist." Miles disagrees, slamming Hurley's Michael J. Fox–inspired theory, explaining, "It doesn't work like that. You can't change anything. Your maniac Iraqi buddy shot Linus. That is what always happened. It's just . . . we never experienced how it all turns out."

Did you follow that, or did you have to hit rewind on your TiVo? Hurley is confused, and so are we. The logic will keep you running in circles. Everything that happens and every word the Losties speak is actually something they already did, a word they already spoke in the past— they just can't remember it. Hmm . . . maybe a speeding DeLorean with a flux capacitor *does* make more sense. Hurley, then, makes the inevitable connection: what if one of them dies . . . in the past? That would most certainly change the realities of the future. Right? Right? Well, not necessarily. Miles breaks it down for us: "I can die because I've already come to the island on the freighter.

Any of us can die because this is our present." So our time travelers are living in their present and interacting with others who are existing in their pasts.

Make sense now? In other words, while a twelve-year-old Ben Linus is a manifestation of the past for Hurley and Miles, the grown-up Ben is also living his own present, and it is *not* in the 1970s with Hurley and Miles. He has not traveled back in time—he is currently on the island with Locke (or unLocke, if you will) in *his* present. But Hurley zeroes in on another fault line in this theory as he remembers the Losties' first interaction with Ben: "When we first captured Ben, and Sayid, like, tortured him, then why wouldn't he remember getting shot by that same guy when he was a kid?" He has a point.

It all seems confusing, but one thing is certain: change is not possible. Whatever happened, happened—period. Unless . . . ? Well, unless it did not. In these scenarios we lean on the brightest mind among us. Daniel Faraday is a brilliant young scientist with a mind that is capable of seeing the complexities of the world. He alone among the Losties is capable of locating and navigating the loopholes of the natural order. But at the end of the day, even Faraday is left with more mystery than ever. The universe will never be fully mastered or understood. Created by a God with so much creativity and power, our minds can only take in small portions of its beauty. What are we to do when we reach these inevitable roadblocks to understanding? In the words of Faraday: "That's where we leave science behind." I agree.

It seems that too often we have become too smart for our own good, believing that we understand the secrets of the universe. How is life conceived? How is it that seed and soil form a perfect union and give birth to the food that nourishes our body? How do we imagine the vastness of the universe as we reside on a relatively small planet in an under-sized galaxy known as the Milky Way? Some claim these grand mysteries are predictable and explainable. After all, we can take the elemental forms of life and create an embryo in the laboratory that can result in the birth of a child, we alter the genetic code of almost every plant and seed to produce crops to our specification, and we seem to be the only life-form exploring the vastness of space. Honest scientific inquiry will always acknowledge, as Daniel Faraday does, that at the limits of our understanding there must be something much greater at work. In these moments we see God most clearly. Imagine the awe and wonder God's children experienced as they witnessed one supernatural event after another pry them from the oppressive hands of Pharaoh and propel them out of slavery in Egypt so that God might sustain them in the wilderness. What might it have been like to hold in your hands a bread that fell from the heavens? They named that bread *manna*—a Hebrew word that means "what is this?" You can imagine that with every bite, they grew in their sense of wonder at the ways God chose to provide for their every need. We feel as though we are more independent, but the air that we breathe, the food that sustains us, and the children who bless us are no less gifts from God.

My friend Kyle Lake expressed this sentiment beautifully in the conclusion to a sermon he was to preach on October 30, 2005. Kyle was a dear friend who served with me as an associate pastor at the church I founded in Waco, Texas, known as University Baptist. As I moved on to the greener, more humid pastures of Houston, Kyle became the lead pastor. On this particular Sunday, he led the church in the celebration of the baptism of several young people. In a tragic turn of events, Kyle was electrocuted and killed during the baptismal service. He did not preach that morning, but this is the conclusion to his sermon that was found tucked carefully in his Bible:

Live. And Live Well.

Breathe. Breathe in and breathe deeply. Be *present*. Do not be past. Do not be future. Be now.

On a crystal clear, breezy seventy-degree day, roll down the windows and *feel* the wind against your skin. Feel the warmth of the sun.

If you run, then allow those first few breaths on a

cool autumn day to *freeze* your lungs and do not just be alarmed, be *alive*.

Get knee-deep in a novel and *lose* track of time.

If you bike, pedal *hard* . . . and if you crash, then crash well.

Feel the *satisfaction* of a job well done—a paper well written, a project thoroughly completed, a play well performed.

If you must wipe the snot from your three-year old's nose, don't be disgusted if the Kleenex didn't catch it all . . . because soon he'll be wiping his own.

If you've recently experienced loss, then *grieve*. And grieve well.

At the table with friends and family, *laugh*. If you're eating and laughing at the same time, then you might as well laugh until you puke. And if you eat, then *smell*. The aromas are not impediments to your day. Steak on the grill, coffee beans freshly ground, cookies in the oven. And *taste*. Taste every ounce of flavor. Taste every ounce of friendship. Taste every ounce of life. Because it is most definitely a gift.[1]

Epilogue

Writing *The Gospel According to Lost* has been a pleasure for me. I love these stories and the way people interact with them. There is a sense of respect and camaraderie among people who love this show. It's true I do get some odd looks and spirited resistance from the religious establishment at times when I tell them that I hear God speak to me through the popular culture. They struggle to understand, as some can hardly imagine that echoes of Jesus can be heard in the voices of Jack Shephard or Hugo "Hurley" Reyes, much less someone like Charles Widmore. But I am not sure that this kind of book is vastly different from the ways that Jesus taught his disciples; they simply walked through life together—eating, traveling, fishing, farming—and as they lived life, Jesus drew spiritual insights from these activities. He taught them to pursue and love people as fishers of men, and to be aware that our actions have profound effects by explaining the simple principle that we will always reap what we sow.

Lost is filled with spiritual, historical, philosophical, and scientific insights. However, the truth is we watch it because it is just plain fun. I sometimes wonder if I wrote this book so that I could have a legitimate reason to rewatch *Lost* episodes while my wife put the kids to bed. Honestly, that may be part of the motivation. But ultimately I come alive when I experience great art that connects me with the world and its people on a much deeper level—and *Lost* does that for me.

We have one season left on this epic journey, and I would love to leave you with a few parting thoughts about how we might experience season six well:

Build Community

Invite as many new friends as possible over to experience this journey and share these conversations. Because the cast of characters on this show is so diverse, it allows us to build far-reaching connections and make new friends. Do you have Korean neighbors? Ask them to bring some kimchi (that stuff is good) to your *Lost* party and make new friends. Historically television has been targeted to specific ethnic groups; in the world of satellite televisions and millions of choices, most people are looking to embrace shows with a cast of characters that look and sound like they do. Again, this is just another indication that *Lost* has broken the mold.

Celebrate

Enjoy this last season with good food and truly make it a party. There could be nothing finer than to bake up some ziti or grill some steaks to add some flavor to an episode we have anticipated for months. In a world filled with greed and fear, good food connects us to the earth and our Creator. As we experience it together, it lifts us beyond our miniscule part of the world and helps us to see beyond our struggles and selfishness. J. R. R. Tolkien wrote, "If more of us valued food and cheer and song above hoarded gold, it would be a merrier world."[1]

Learn

Experience *Lost* on every level. Allow yourself to be moved emotionally, but then take the time to contemplate the narrative on a deeper plane. If we truly allow ourselves to learn from this show, it will lead us to change some things. We may see that we are every bit as controlling as Benjamin Linus (God forbid)—but if this is true, we have many people waiting for an apology, so we should seek them out and start again with a *tabula rasa* (clean slate).

Show Gratitude

If we look carefully at what we are attracted to in each and every character, we may find that the common thread is the ways the island has softened them—that after the crash they became much more likable than their old selves. They continue to struggle, but they have learned to appreciate life in a new way; they seem to smile more often on the island than they ever do in their flashbacks.

The truth is, our lives are filled with as much mystery as this show—none of us knows what happens next. We long to understand, but ultimately we are left with anticipation. Our future is as unknown as the time that Jesus will return to this earth to establish his kingdom: according to Jesus, only the Father knows the time his Son will enter this created order once again. But we are not aimless people stumbling in the dark. We are not lost. We know what it is that we are to do each day; Jesus called it the greatest commandment to love God and our neighbor. We have no answers in regard to the *how* or the *when*, but the question of *what* it is that we are to be doing was answered long ago.

Notes

Prologue

1. All quotations, dialog, and excerpts contained in this book are taken from the author's transcription of Seasons 1 through 7 of the *Lost* DVD Series.

Chapter 1: Embracing the Mystery

1. Albert Einstein, in the lecture "What I Believe," 1930.
2. "J. J. Abrams' mystery box," TED Conference, March 2007; available at www.ted.com/talks/j_j_abrams_mystery_box.html.
3. Frederick Buechner, *Secrets in the Dark* (New York: HarperCollins, 2007).
4. Annie Dillard, *Pilgrim at Tinker Creek* (New York: Harper's Magazine Press, 1974; New York: HarperCollins, 1999), 3.

Chapter 2: Life as Backgammon

1. From the play fragment *The Sons of Aleus*.
2. Friedrich Nietzsche, *Beyond Good and Evil* (1886).

Chapter 3: Numbers Don't Lie—Hurley: Patron Saint of Blessed Losers

1. Paulo Coelho, *The Alchemist* (New York: HarperCollins, 2006).

Notes

Chapter 4: Sayid Jarrah: Patron Saint of Tormented Humanitarians

1. Chris Carabott, "Lost: 'The Economist' Review," 15 February 2008, IGN Entertainment, Inc., www.tv.ign.com/articles/852/852545p1.html?RSSwhen2008-02-15_100200&RSSid=852545 (accessed 21 July 2009).

Chapter 7: Man of Science, Man of Faith: Saint Jack and Saint John

1. James Poniewozik, "Lostwatch: I gotta have faith," *Time*, 25 February 2009, available online at tunedin.blogs.time.com/2009/02/25/lostwatch-i-gotta-have-faith/ (accessed 20 August 2009).
2. William Kingdon Clifford, *The Ethics of Belief and Other Essays* (1879; repr., Amherst: Prometheus, 1999) 77.

Chapter 8: Locke and the Island: John Locke (1632–1704)

1. John Locke and Victor Nuovo, *John Locke: Writings on Religion* (Oxford: Oxford University Press, 2002), xiii.

Chapter 10: Jesus Wrote a Best Seller

1. Brennan Manning, *The Ragamuffin Gospel* (Colorado Springs: Multnomah Books, 1993).

Chapter 11: Eko: Patron Saint of Warlord Priests

1. Jennifer Armstrong, "The Tailie's End," *Entertainment Weekly* online, www.ew.com/ew/article/0,,1553848,00.html (accessed 21 August 2009).
2. Gilda Radner, *It's Always Something*, repr. ed. (1989; repr., New York: Harper, 2000), 237.

Notes

Chapter 14: Benjamin Linus: Patron Saint of Dutiful Tyrants

1. *Bono: In Conversation with Michka Assayas* (Riverhead, 2005).

Chapter 15: Jacob: Patron Saint of Fathers

1. D. H. Lawrence, *Apocalypse and the Writings on Revelation* (1931; repr., London: Penguin, 1995) 144.

Chapter 17: Daniel Faraday: Patron Saint of Mystic Scientists

1. Reprinted with permission.

Epilogue

1. Spoken by Thorin Oakenshield to Bilbo Baggins in *The Hobbit* (New York: Houghton Mifflin, 1937) 299.

A Project to Rediscover the Bible

The Scripture quotations in *The Gospel According to Lost* have been taken from *The Voice™*.

A collaboration between scholars, writers, musicians, and other artists to bring the Bible to life.

The Voice™ is a fresh expression of the timeless narrative known as the Bible. Too often the passion, grit, humor, and beauty has been lost in the translation process. *The Voice™* seeks to recapture what was lost.

To learn more, visit www.hearthevoice.com.

Available wherever books & Bibles are sold

More from Chris Seay

Blog: www.therestorativejustice.org
Twitter: PastorChrisSeay
Church/ Podcasts: www.ecclesiahouston.org

The images in *The Gospel According to Lost*
are original paintings by Scott Erickson,
studio artist and experiential artist in
residence at Ecclesia Church in Houston.

To purchase prints of the Saints of Lost
paintings featured in this book, or learn more
about Scott and his work,
visit www.thetranspireproject.com.